Austin mini
Metro

All Metro models:

Standard, City, L and HLE, 998 cc
1.3L, 1.3S, 1.3HL and 1.3HLS, 1275 cc
MG and Vanden Plas, 1275 cc

Owner's Handbook/Servicing Guide

by Ian Coomber

ABCDE
FGHIJ
KLMNO
PQRST

Haynes

THE
BOOK

Acknowledgements

Thanks are due to many people for their assistance to the author and publishers during the preparation of this Handbook. Advice on lubrication was given by Castrol Ltd, and on spark plugs by the Champion Sparking Plug Company. Special thanks are due to Nelson and Sally James, whose Metro appears on the front cover of this Handbook.

A book in the Haynes Owner's Handbook/Servicing Guide Series.

© Haynes Publishing Group 1983

Printed and published by the Haynes Publishing Group, Sparkford, Yeovil, Somerset BA22 7JJ

ISBN 0 85696 804 8

Although every care has been taken to ensure the correctness of data used, it must be borne in mind that alterations and design changes can occur within the production run of a model without specific reclassification. No liability can be accepted for damage, loss or injury caused by errors or omissions in the information given.

Contents

MG Metro – the latest in the range

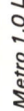

Metro 1.0 L

Metro 1.3 HLS

What's in it for You?

Whether you've bought this book yourself or had it given to you, the idea was probably the same in either case — to help you get the best out of your Metro and perhaps to make your motoring a bit less of a drain on your hard-earned cash at the same time.

Garage labour charges can easily be several times your own hourly rate of pay, and usually form the main part of any servicing bill; we'll help you avoid them by carrying out the routine services yourself. Even if you *don't* want to do the regular servicing, and prefer to leave it to your Leyland dealer, there are some things you should check regularly just to make sure that your car's not a danger to you or to anyone else on the road; we tell you what they are.

If you're about to start doing your own servicing (whether to cut costs or to be sure that it's done properly) we think you'll find the procedures described give an easy-to-follow introduction to what can be a very satisfying way of spending a few hours of your spare time.

We've included some tips that should save you money when buying replacement parts and even while you're driving; there's a chapter on cleaning and renovating your car, and another on fitting accessories.

Apart from the things every Metro owner needs to know to deal with mishaps like a puncture or a broken headlamp, we've put together some Trouble-shooter Charts to cover the more likely of the problems that can crop up with even the most carefully maintained car sooner or later.

There's also a set of conversion tables, a section explaining the sort of jargon used by experts (and not-so-experts!) when talking about cars, and a comprehensive alphabetical index to help you find your way round the book.

If the bug gets you, and you're keen to tackle some of the more advanced repair jobs on your car, then you'll need our Owner's Workshop Manual for the Metro models, which gives a step-by-step guide to all the repair and overhaul tasks on these cars, with plenty of illustrations to make things even clearer.

The Metro Family

The Austin mini Metro was introduced in October 1980. Although entering the highly competitive corner of the compact family saloon market, its distinctive looks combined with a long pedigree soon enabled it to carve itself a sizeable niche in the market place.

The initial range of models consisted of a low compression fleet option, Standard and L versions, and the economy HLE version, all being fitted with a 998 cc engine. Sporty 1.3 S (later HL) and luxury HLS models were also available, both being fitted with the 1275 cc engine. These early models were all fitted with a four-speed manual transmission. The body is of two-door plus hatchback design.

It should be mentioned that whilst the 'A-plus' engine and gearbox units are similar to those fitted to the BL Mini, the later units are much improved, durability and economy being prime considerations. Drive from the transmission is taken through the front wheels and the engine/gearbox unit is fitted transversely across the front of the car.

The most significant design characteristics are bolt-on front wings, self-cleaning distributor contact points, fully closed crankcase ventilation system, front-mounted aluminium radiator, dual circuit braking system, and Hydragas suspension. Instrumentation is comprehensive, even on the basic models, and includes a seat belt warning lamp, brake pad wear warning lamp, and handbrake warning lamp.

Since the Metro's original introduction, further models and variations have been introduced. In February 1981 an L version powered by the 1.3 engine became available, similar in other respects to the 1.0 engine L version. Availability was at first limited to fleet users. A four-speed automatic transmission became available for the 1.3 engine range in July 1981.

The smaller-engined range had the Metro City variant added to it in February 1982, whilst in May of that year, the controversial MG Metro was added to the 1.3 range of models. Called badge engineering by the purists, it nevertheless has its own distinguishing features, such as a 72 bhp power unit giving it a top speed of just over 100 mph, a rear window spoiler and a set of distinctive alloy 'sports' wheels.

Another model which has been added to the range is the Metro Vanden Plas, also fitted with the 1.3 litre engine. This is the most luxurious model available in the range of Metros and includes features such as a glass sun roof, wood door cappings and Raschelle fabric trim.

Specification details are given in *Vital Statistics*, but the following summary gives details of the major changes in the range of models.

Austin mini Metro

October 1980	Range introduced. 998 cc or 1275 cc, choice of 5 models from Standard to HLS
February 1981	1.3L version available to fleet users
July 1981	Automatic transmission version available with 1.3 engine
February 1982	Metro City added to 1-litre range
April 1982	Vanden Plas model available
May 1982	MG Metro added to 1.3 range
September 1982	1.3L version available to public. 1.3HL replaces 1.3S; trim improvements to most models

Road Test Data taken from

The figures published here are extracts from *Autocar* magazine road tests.

Fuel consumption: The mpg figure is the overall consumption figure for their test period, including performance testing. Many owners will achieve significantly better consumption figures. The formula on the right provides a guide ('**mpg**' refers to the quoted overall test figure).

	severe	average	easy
Driving conditions			
Driving style			
Hard	−10%	**mpg**	+10%
Average	+10%	+20%	
Gentle		+20%	+30%

	Metro Standard	Metro 1.3 HLS	Metro Automatic	MG Metro 1300
Maximum speed (mph)	84	94	89	100
Overall fuel consumption (mpg)	35.2	31.3	27.7	38.8
Fuel consumption (mpg) at constant:				
30 mph	67.4	71.0	44.4	60.5
50 mph	50.8	48.9	42.4	48.7
70 mph	35.4	38.0	32.8	35.2
Range on full fuel tank (miles)	232	207	183	256
Acceleration (seconds):				
0–30 mph	4.6	4.0	6.8	3.5
0–40 mph	8.3	6.0	9.7	5.8
0–50 mph	13.1	9.1	13.8	8.2
0–60 mph	18.9	13.5	19.4	12.2
0–70 mph	30.6	18.2	28.3	16.9
Standing start ¼ mile	21.6	19.2	22.1	18.6
40–60 mph in normal top gear	15.5	11.9	(10.8 in 3rd)	11.2

In the driving seat

Most experienced drivers will probably be able to sit in the driving seat of the Metro for the first time and be familiar immediately with the instruments and controls and their usage.

Many people however, especially those not acquainted with the Metro, will need to take stock of the various controls and their functions. The layout of all models is fairly straightforward, but a little information on one or two things may be useful if only to clarify their use.

The instrument panel

The layout and composition of the instrument panel depends on the model in question. Whatever type you have in your Metro, the functions and any special notes regarding the instruments and warning lights are given below.

Speedometer

This instrument incorporates a total mileage indicator. The trip meter can be reset by means of the reset knob and can be useful in checking the fuel consumption over a recorded mileage.

Fuel and temperature gauge

The operation of both these gauges is self-evident. With the fuel gauge, the pointer will indicate the approximate amount of fuel in the tank, but only when the ignition is switched on. When the pointer drops into the red sector, the fuel level is low and should be topped up. The true reading of fuel level on the gauge is reached after the ignition has remained on for 30 seconds.

With regard to the temperature gauge, the pointer should, when the engine is warmed up, rest midway between the red (hot) and blue (cold) sectors. If the weather's particularly hot and/or you're in a traffic jam or climbing mountain roads, then the needle may advance slightly more than usual towards the hot position (red sector). If however at any time the needle starts to rise rapidly to, or has reached, the red sector, then stop the engine and carefully investigate the cause. The main causes are usually (a) loose or broken water pump/alternator drivebelt, (b) loss of coolant, (c) faulty thermostat, or (d) a faulty electric cooling fan.

If on investigation the electric cooling fan is found to be operational, then check items (a) and (b), but note that extra care must be taken when checking the coolant level when the engine is hot – see *Filling Station Facts* for the right way to do it. Adjustment or renewal of the water pump/alternator drivebelt is given in *Service Scene*.

If the cooling fan is not working, then a basic check should be made to ensure that the wiring connections to the fan unit and the thermostatic switch on the radiator are securely made. You can drive safely without the cooling fan working as long as the temperature gauge stays out of the red zone.

Tachometer (where fitted)

This instrument records the engine speed by means of electrical impulses and is useful as a means of preventing over-revving of the engine in the intermediate gears. The maximum safe engine speed is 5500 rpm. The needle should not be allowed to enter the red zone on the gauge in any gear.

Clock

The standard type clock fitted to such models as the HLE operates automatically except when the battery is disconnected. To reset the hands, simply push the control knob in and turn it as required.

On some models the tachometer also includes a digital clock, which is adjustable by means of the control on the front face of the gauge. To adjust the minute display, the control must be turned anti-clockwise (against spring pressure) in the direction of the arrow towards the 'M' marking, whilst to adjust the hour reading the control is turned clockwise towards the 'H' marking. The clock can also be zeroed **11**

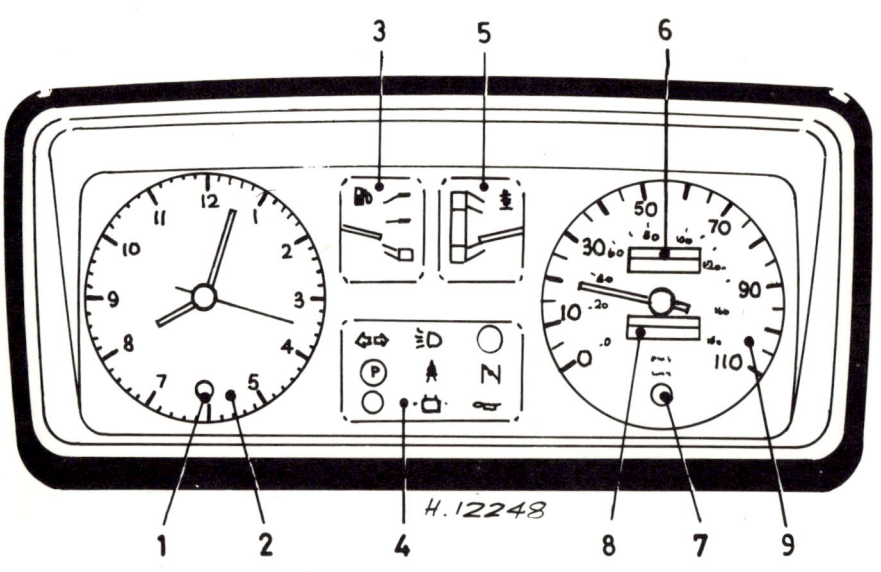

Instrument panel layout – L and HLE models

1	Clock reset button	4	Warning lights panel	7	Trip mileage reset button
2	Clock	5	Coolant temperature gauge	8	Trip meter
3	Fuel gauge	6	Milometer	9	Speedometer

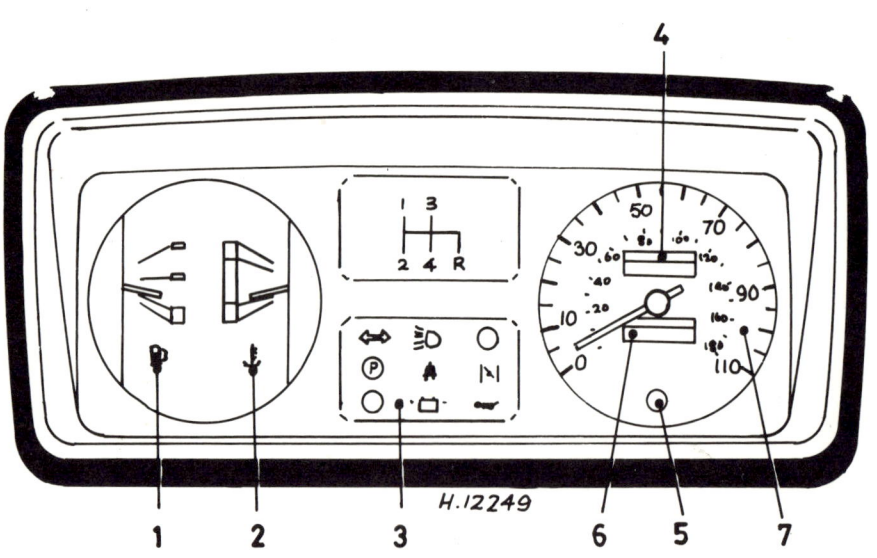

Instrument panel layout – City/Standard models

1	Fuel gauge	4	Milometer	6	Trip meter
2	Coolant temperature gauge	5	Trip mileage reset button	7	Speedometer
3	Warning lights panel				

Typical instrument panel layout for Metro 1.3S, HL, HLS, Vanden Plas and MG models

1   Tachometer
2   Digital clock and reset button
3   Warning lights panel
4   Fuel gauge
5   Coolant temperature gauge
6   Speedometer
7   Milometer
8   Trip meter
9   Trip meter reset button

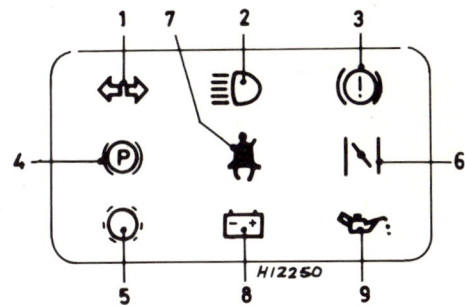

Instrument panel warning lights

1   Indicator warning light
2   Main beam warning light
3   Brake fluid level warning light
4   Handbrake warning light
5   Brake disc pad wear warning light
6   Mixture control (choke) warning light
7   Seat belt warning light
8   Ignition (no-charge) warning light
9   Oil pressure warning light

by turning the control clockwise, but to its second stop position. The clock is designed so that it will illuminate even when the ignition is switched off.

Cigar lighter

To operate the cigar lighter, push the holder into the socket, then release it. When the lighter has reached the required temperature the holder will pop out to the extended position ready to use. It usually takes about fifteen seconds for the lighter to fully heat up.

Choke control

The manually operated choke should only be used for starting the engine when cold. The control knob should be pulled out fully and the engine started without touching the accelerator pedal. Once the engine has started, the choke should be used only as long as is necessary for the engine to run smoothly without stalling. Progressively push the control knob back into the dash panel as the engine warms up to its normal operating temperature.

An amber 'choke on' warning light will illuminate as a reminder whilst the choke is in use (ignition on).

Warning lights

The warning lights are situated in the main instrument cluster. By reference to the illustrations the function of most will be seen to be self-evident. However, one or two need slight elaboration.

Ignition warning light

This serves the dual purpose of reminding the driver that the ignition circuit is switched on (even though the engine may not be running), as well as acting as a no-charge indicator. It should light up when the ignition is switched on, and may also be on when the engine is idling, but should go out at any engine speed above idling. If this doesn't happen,

you've probably got a problem on your hands which needs pretty urgent attention.

Oil pressure warning light

This light should only be on when the ignition is switched on, and should go out as soon as the engine is running. If it doesn't go out until several seconds after start-up, it suggests that the engine oil level is very low, or a considerable degree of wear exists somewhere in the engine, or (less likely) that some of the oilways are blocked. If the engine oil level is correct then the last two faults can possibly be lived with for a while, but expect problems in the not too distant future!

If the warning light comes on while you're travelling, *switch off the engine immediately*. It could

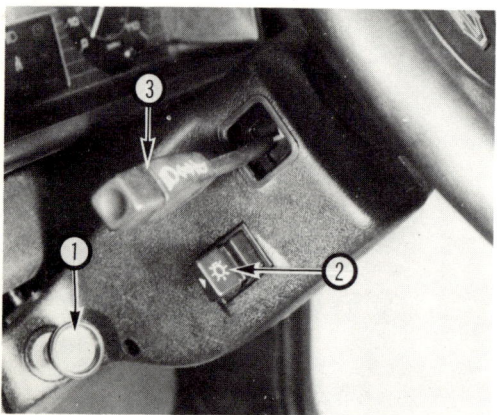

View showing the choke control knob (1), the light switch (2) and the headlight dip/flash, horn and direction indicator switch (3)

be a duff switch, but more likely you're out of oil or the lubrication system has failed, and that's serious. If you can't find the cause, get expert assistance – but **don't** drive the car.

Brake fluid level warning light

This warning light should only light up when the ignition key is turned to operate the starter motor (position III). If it doesn't, then it is indicative of a faulty bulb or wiring, and this should be checked without delay.

Should this warning light illuminate at any other time when driving, it indicates that a fault exists in the brake hydraulic circuits, causing the fluid level in the master cylinder reservoir to drop below its normal safe level. The fluid level should be checked on a weekly basis as described in *Service Scene*, so if the light comes on either you have been neglecting this task, or the fluid level has dropped rapidly due to a leak in the hydraulic system. In either case the fluid level in the reservoir should be topped up and a thorough check of the brake hydraulic circuits made to find the cause of the problem.

The Metro is fitted with a dual circuit brake system, so should a fault develop in the front circuit, then the rear circuit remains operational and vice versa. If you are unlucky enough to suffer a failure in one circuit, remember that whilst you can still drive the car, the braking efficiency will be greatly reduced and a longer pedal travel will be required before the free play is taken up. Pumping the pedal will not restore the pressure. The fault *must* be repaired at the very earliest opportunity.

Brake pad wear warning light

Should the brake pad wear warning light come on during braking, it is indicative that the front brake disc pads have worn down to the minimum thickness permissible and they must therefore be renewed at the earliest opportunity. Details are given in *Service Scene*.

Switches

Ignition/starter switch and steering column lock

This switch has four key positions and these are marked 0 to III. The function of each is as follows:

'0'   This is the lock positon. When the key's in this position the column may be locked by turning the steering wheel until it's felt to click into position.

I   When unlocking the steering the key must be turned from the '0' position to 'I'. It may be necessary to 'rock' the steering wheel to ease the key movement to this position. If the vehicle's ever towed the key must be in this position.

II   In this position the ignition is on.

III   To operate the starter the key must be moved from the 'II' position to 'III', and then when the engine starts up, the key is released and returns under spring tension to the II (ignition on) position.

Note: Door and ignition keys are easily and often lost. This can be inconvenient and embarrassing and it therefore pays to carry a spare just in case! The number of the key should be noted and kept in a safe place for reference since the lock has no identification number stamped on it. If you're ever caught in this predicament you should contact the AA/RAC, your local Leyland dealer or the police who may be able to assist you to 'enter without breaking'.

Headlight dip/flash, horn and direction indicator switch

This stalk type switch is on the left-hand side of the steering column. It controls three functions when moved in line with the column, these being (1) to operate the headlight main beams – push fully forwards towards the dashboard; (2) to operate the headlights on dipped beams – switch in central position and (3) to operate the headlight flasher – pull the switch upwards towards the steering wheel against the return spring pressure. The last function will operate the headlights whether the main light switch is on or off.

To operate the horn, press the lever end button inwards (towards the column).

To operate the indicators, move the lever down-

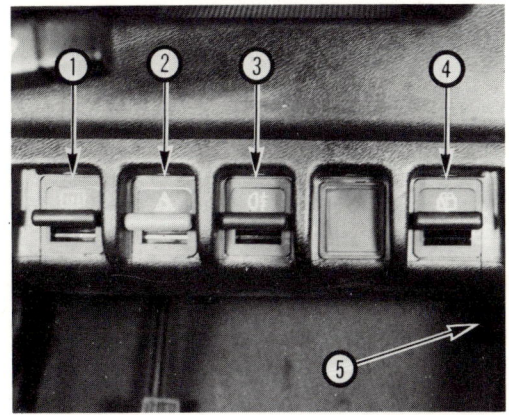

The facia panel switches

1   Rear window demister switch
2   Hazard warning switch
3   Rear foglight switch
4   Rear window washer/wiper switch
5   Bonnet release is located under the panel

wards for a left turn or upwards for a right turn. When operated, the green warning light will flash on and off until the switch returns to the neutral position.

Windscreen wiper/washer and headlamp washer switch

This switch is found on the right-hand side of the steering column. From the neutral position, raise the lever one notch to set the windscreen wipers at the standard speed. For the fast wipe speed raise the lever to the second notch position. A third function is achieved by pressing the lever downwards against the spring pressure to provide a single sweep wipe of the screen.

To operate the windscreen washer, press the button on the end of the lever inwards (towards the column). This will also operate the headlamp washers, where fitted, but only when the headlamps are on.

Side and headlight switch

Located on the left-hand side of the steering column, moving the switch upwards towards the wheel to position one operates the side and tail lights. To operate the headlights, pull the switch up to position two. When the switch is activated the green warning light on the instrument panel will glow.

Rear window wiper/washer switch (where fitted)

This is a two-stage rocker switch. Press it down to stage one to operate the wiper, and fully down to stage two to operate the washer.

Rear window demister switch

Press this switch down to operate the rear window demister, but only leave it in the 'on' position (indicated by the amber warning light on the switch

itself) just as long as is necessary to clear the glass. The demister will not operate when the ignition is switched off.

Rear foglight switch

The rear foglight will only operate when the headlights are switched on. Push the switch knob down for 'on'. An amber warning light in the switch itself will glow to indicate that it is switched on.

Hazard flasher

Marked with a safety triangle, this switch will operate all direction indicator lights simultaneously when switched on. Press the switch button down for 'on' and up for 'off'. The hazard flasher is designed to work with the ignition switched on or off.

Heating and ventilation controls

The heating and ventilation system of the car is operated by the controls situated in the centre of the dashboard, and by the various vents/outlets.

Face level ventilation control

Referring to the photo, the control lever (2) adjusts the quantity of fresh air flow through the air vents. The vents are adjustable for direction by sliding the control knob (3) in the direction required.

Blower fan

A two-speed blower fan is fitted. It can only be operated when the ignition key is set in positions I or II. The blower must not be used when the control levers are set at the 'OFF' position.

Temperature control

The temperature control is located to the right of the ventilation control grille. Sliding the control lever up towards the blue marking provides cool air, whilst sliding the control downwards to the red mark provides hot air. Hot air will not be available until the engine has warmed up!

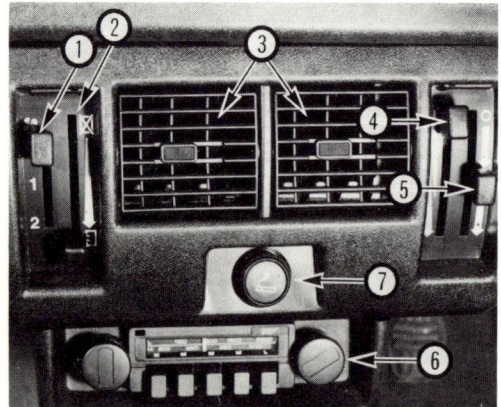

Air distribution control

On the extreme right side of the panel is the air distribution control. When located centrally it provides airflow to the windscreen (for demisting), whilst full downwards movement of the lever diverts the airflow to both windscreen and car interior.

Trip computer

Only available on some models, the device enables the driver to monitor average speeds, journey times and fuel consumption. This is particularly useful in that the driver can instantly analyse his or her driving, and the car's performance, relative to the journey in question and the conditions prevailing. Speed can then be adjusted with regard to time and economy.

The device is shown in the accompanying diagram, and its functions are as follows.

Display panel

Provides the display of information whenever a function button is pressed. To the right of the display panel is the metric/Imperial display button. The function readout can be given in either metric or Imperial readings as required by simply sliding the button to the left (metric) or right (Imperial). Individual function readings will remain set unless a further function button is pressed.

Elapsed time function (E/T)

To operate this function, press the 'Clear' button at the start of a journey. The time taken for the journey will then be recorded. During the first hour the reading will be given in minutes and seconds. After the first hour the reading will be given in hours and minutes.

Distance travelled function (DIST)

16   This function enables a journey distance to be

The heater controls, ventilation controls and radio

1   Blower fan control
2   Ventilation (face level) control
3   Air vents with direction controls
4   Temperature control
5   Air distribution (windscreen or interior) control
6   Radio location (standard position when fitted)
7   Cigar lighter location (where fitted)

recorded, and the distance travelled displayed at any stage of the journey.

Average speed (AVE·SPD)

This function when pressed gives a readout of the average speed being taken during the journey.

Fuel function button (FUEL)

When this button is pressed, the trip fuel consumption readout (total fuel used) will be given.

Instant fuel (INST)

Pressing this button provides the driver with the fuel consumption at the time of pressing the button. It should be noted that if this button is pressed when vehicle speed is below 5 mph, the display will be flashed in gal/hour or litres/hour as applicable. In any case, the figure given depends on the driving conditions and the throttle opening at the time. This reading will not therefore be an average fuel consumption.

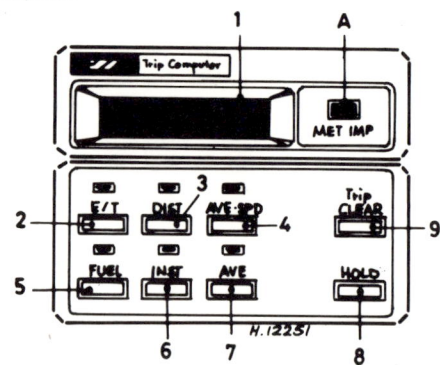

The trip computer controls

1   Display (read-out) with metric or imperial reading button (A)
2   Elapsed time
3   Distance travelled
4   Average speed
5   Fuel used (total)
6   Fuel consumption at time of pressing button
7   Average journey fuel consumption
8   Hold
9   Clear or reset button

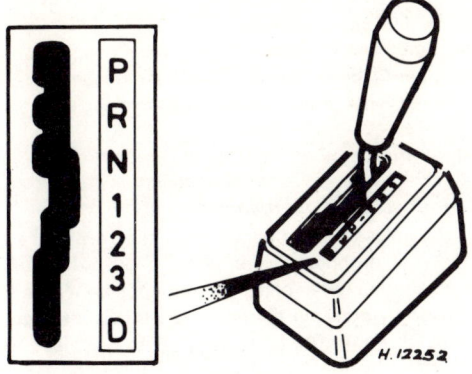

The automatic transmission selector positions

P	Park
R	Reverse
N	Neutral
1	Low gear
2	2nd gear
3	3rd gear
D	Drive

Average fuel (AVE)

This function will provide a read-out of the total journey fuel consumption at the time of pressing the button.

Hold function (HOLD)

This button when pressed enables all functions to be suspended during a stop or extended delay during a journey. To reactivate the functions when the journey is restarted, simply press the 'Hold' button again.

Clear (Trip CLEAR)

Hold this button in for two seconds to enable the trip computer to clear itself of information compiled previously.

Automatic transmission

The automatic transmission incorporates four forward speeds and one reverse speed; speeds 1, 2, and 3 may be selected and held independently of the automatic function. A torque converter transmits drive from the engine to the transmission.

Controls

The floor mounted selector lever is moved manually through its quadrant to any one of the seven marked positions, the functions of which are as follows:

'P' (Park) – In this position with the engine either stopped or running, no gears are engaged and the gearbox output shaft is mechanically locked, which in effect means that the driving wheels are also locked, and the car cannot be moved. The engine may be started in this position. Don't select 'P' if the car is moving, or damage will result.

'R' (Reverse) – Reverse gear position. It is most important that this gear must only be selected when the car is stationary.

'N' (Neutral) – The conditions for neutral are the same as for 'P' except that the gearbox output shaft is not mechanically locked. The car will, therefore, roll with the engine either running or stopped unless the handbrake (or footbrake) is applied.

'1' (Low gear) – First gear manual hold, for selection when the car is stationary. This is a freewheel gear, not having any engine braking effect, and is therefore of no assistance when descending steep hills. Under no circumstances must this gear be selected at any speed above 30 mph (56 km/h).

'2' (2nd) – Second gear manual hold. Can be selected to provide engine braking on downhill gradients, but must not be selected at any speed over 50 mph (80 km/h).

'3' (3rd) – Third gear manual hold. Can be selected to provide moderate engine braking on downhill gradients, but must not be selected at any speed over 70 mph (113 km/h). Do not drive away from rest in this gear.

'D' (Drive) – Automatic gear changes. This is the selector position for normal driving requirements. In this position, first gear's initially engaged but, with engine idling, the brakes off, the car may creep forward. The engine can't be started in this position. With the engine speed increased, the car will move forward in low gear. When the speed and load conditions are right, the transmission will automatically move up through the gears. When speed decreases, the gears will automatically shift back down as far as first, again according to speed and load situations.

Control techniques with an automatic transmission

This transmission type can be used either as a fully automatic transmission in which all forward speeds can change up and down automatically, or as a manual change gearbox with certain limitations. Reverse gear must always be selected manually and with the car stationary.

When using the gearbox manually it's most important that the gearchanges are made at the correct road speeds or serious damage to the trans- **17** mission will result. The recommended speed ranges for each gear are as follows:

1st – 0 to 30 mph (56 km/h)
2nd – 5 to 50 mph (80 km/h)
3rd – 15 to 70 mph (113 km/h)

For normal driving conditions 'D' should be selected, although in cold weather the car should be driven the first few hundred yards in a low gear such as manual 2 to warm the transmission up faster.

To select D or R, first apply the brakes, then move the lever to the required position. Release the brake and accelerate gently, and the car will move in the desired direction. In the D range all changes up and down will be made automatically. The upward changes may be controlled by the accelerator pedal pressure applied. Light pressure ensures that the changes will be made at low road speeds whilst heavy pedal pressure will cause the changes to be made at higher road speeds as desired.

The gearbox will automatically change down on releasing the accelerator pedal pressure and as the car reduces its speed. Upward gear changes take place within the following speed ranges:

1st to 2nd gear – 29 to 37 mph (46 to 59 km/h)
2nd to 3rd gear – 43 to 51 mph (69 to 82 km/h)
3rd to 4th gear – 61 to 69 mph (98 to 111 km/h)

To select a lower gear for overtaking or sudden increase in acceleration, press the pedal down to its fullest extent. When operating this 'kickdown' facility the gear selected will depend on the speed of the car, but it won't operate above the maximum speed specified for the gear. The kick-down speed ranges are as follows:

4th to 3rd gear – 50 to 60 mph (80 to 96 km/h)
3rd to 2nd gear – 40 to 46 mph (64 to 73 km/h)
2nd to 1st gear – 27 to 30 mph (44 to 48 km/h)

Under certain conditions, such as descending steep hills, you may wish to use the gearbox to assist braking, and in this case 2nd or 3rd gear may be selected (but not 1st, as this gear has a freewheel on the overrun). The gears will automatically change down when the speed drops in 'D'.

When stuck: If you manage to get yourself stuck in some mud, sand or snow, try rocking the car back and forth by engaging 'R' and '1' alternately.

Towing with an automatic: It's generally advisable to tow in 'D' range, but when descending steep hills select 2nd or 3rd accordingly.

Being towed: If for any reason you have the misfortune to break down and have to be towed, switch off the ignition, select 'N' and check that the engine oil level's up to the 'Full' mark. Make sure that the handbrake's fully released, and when being towed

the speed should be restricted to 30 mph. Don't tow the car for long distances.

'Creeping': This can occur when a gear's engaged and the engine's idling with the handbrake released. It can be useful when manoeuvring in a confined space.

Miscellaneous

Bonnet release mechanism

To release the bonnet, pull the lever located under the dashboard. The safety catch now visible between the grille panel and bonnet can then be released by pressing the lever upwards to disengage the catch hook. The bonnet can then be raised and supported by the stay provided. Ensure the stay is properly located in the bonnet slot, or you may find the bonnet descending towards your head at a somewhat rapid speed!

When closing the bonnet, release and stow the support stay, lower the bonnet and press it firmly downwards. The safety catch and lock must be heard to engage.

Sunroof

To open the sunroof, grip the handle and push it fully forwards and up to secure the sunroof panel in the open position.

To remove the sunroof panel, open the roof and detach the handle by compressing the link arms together (see illustration), then unclip the safety release spring. Lift the roof panel upwards and to the rear so that the location lugs are clear. The deflector will spring into position automatically.

When refitting the panel, relocate the lugs into position in the roof, also the safety release spring, and then pull the handle to the rear to close the panel.

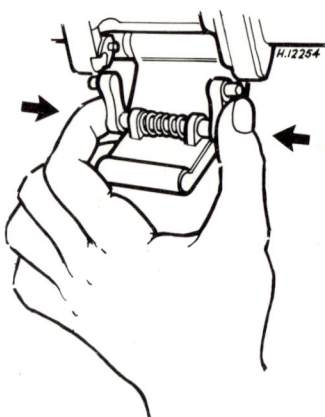

Compress link arms together and detach the safety release spring to lift lugs clear when removing the sunroof

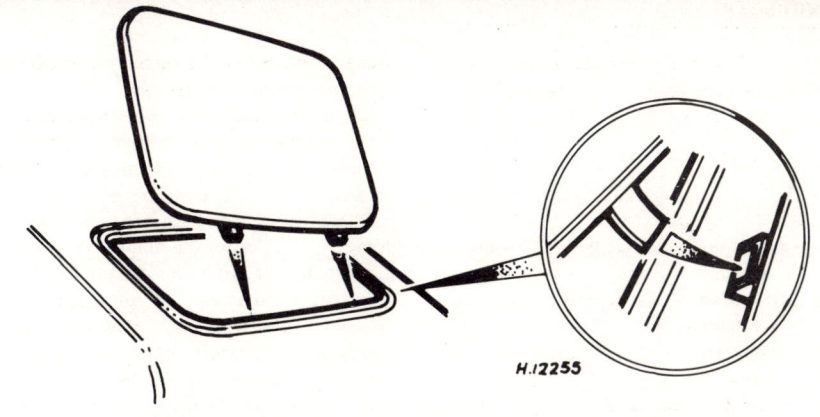

Engage the roof location lugs (inset) when refitting the roof panel

H.12255

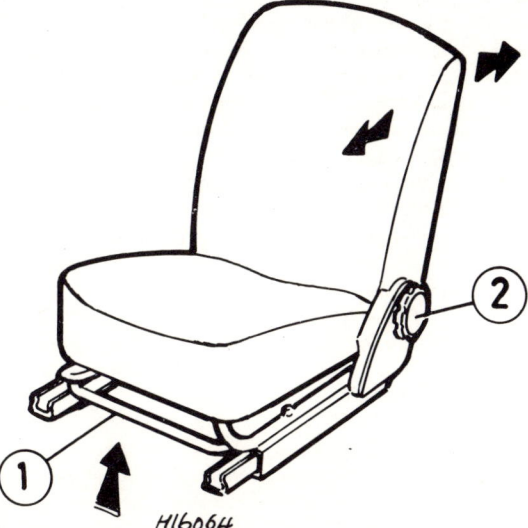

H16064

Seat adjusters (front)

1   Adjuster bar for seat position adjustment
2   Backrest angle adjuster

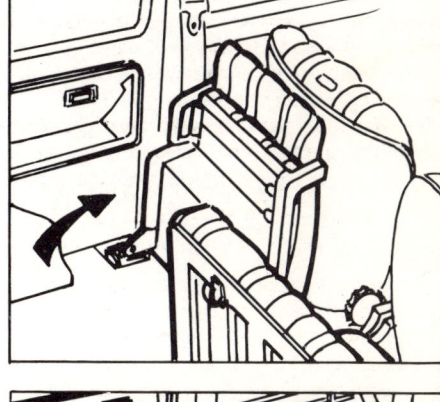

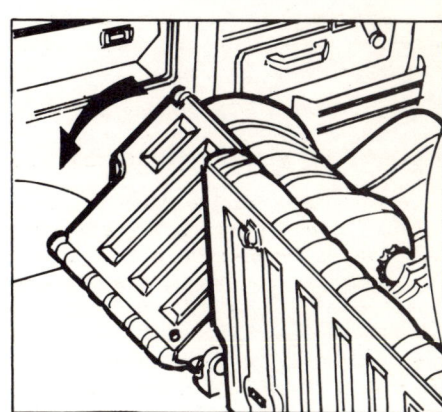

H16066

Two of the rear seat positions possible with the Metro

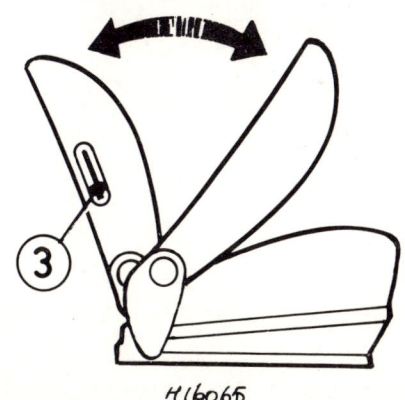

H16065

The front seat back release lever (3)

Interior light

The interior or courtesy light has a three-position switch built into it. The switch functions are as follows:

Switch to rear position – Light comes on automatically when doors are opened and goes off when doors are closed.

Switch in centre – Light is off whether doors are open or not.

Switch to front position – Light comes on irrespective of door positions.

Seats

The front seats are adjustable for backwards-and-forwards movement and for angle of the seat back. To move the seat backwards or forwards, lift the lever under the front of the seat and push or pull as required. The lever should lock itself into the nearest notch when the desired position has been reached.

To alter the angle of the seat back, rotate the knurled wheel situated at the side.

The seat back will also tilt forwards to allow access to the rear by simply raising the release lever on the side and tilting the back forward. On returning the seat back to its normal position, ensure that it is fully locked into position.

The rear seat may be folded down to provide extra carrying capacity in the rear of the car. First it will normally be necessary to remove the rear shelf by removing the elastic strap ends from their locations, then pushing the shelf to the right, disengage the left-hand pivot pin from the hinge, followed by that of the right-hand side. To obtain the maximum possible floor space at the rear, release the rear seat backrest lock (press the levers down) and push the seat back forwards. To secure the rear parcel shelf to the backrest, push the fastener in and turn it in either direction to lock. Fold the backrest together with the seat section forwards.

As an alternative arrangement, the rear seat backrest and seat cushion sections are divided into two sections, so that you can if you wish just fold down the wide or narrow section as required. By folding down the rear backrest on the passenger side and the front passenger seat backrest to the rear, longer than average loads may be carried.

When carrying awkward and/or dirty goods, always try to protect the upholstery by using old blankets or similar to cushion the load.

Filling Station Facts

Whatever else a motorist may choose to ignore when it comes to motoring, a regular visit to a garage for the replenishment of fuel will be necessary, even with the frugal Metro. During such visits the wise motorist will make basic checks to ensure that the engine oil and coolant levels are correct, and also that the tyre pressures are as specified (see the *Quick-Check Chart).* These are items which can easily be overlooked, but which are nevertheless essential maintenance checks and affect the vehicle's safety and reliability.

Whilst the experienced motorist is (or should be) fully aware of these filling station check procedures, the novices to motoring or possibly those who have recently acquired their Metro may need a little guidance. It should be mentioned that these checks are particularly essential when on a long journey, especially on motorways.

As with most things, there's a right and a wrong way to go about the various filling station checks and the following points should be borne in mind when you're carrying them out ...

Checking tyre pressures

Garage tyre pressure gauges are notoriously inaccurate, and it's not really surprising, the way people throw them in a heap on the floor after they've finished with them. This is somewhat disturbing since it's one of the few free services left to motorists and they even abuse that! If facilities exist to hang the line and gauge up then it's a good idea to hang them up out of the way so that the next user doesn't come along and run over the gauge. Of course it isn't always possible to check your pressures at the same garage, so it'll pay to carry a pocket tyre pressure gauge and by using this all the time you'll be certain about any pressure variations.

When checking tyre pressures don't forget to check the pressure in the spare. In the event of a puncture, one flat tyre is a bit of a 'let-down', but having two is really deflating!

Remember that tyre pressures can only be checked accurately when the tyres are cold. Any tyre that's travelled more than a mile or so will show a pressure increase of several pounds per square inch (psi) — maybe more than 5 psi after a longer run. So a certain amount of 'guestimation' comes into checking tyres if they're warm.

Since the pressures won't increase for any reason other than heat the least you can do is to ensure that the pressures in the two front tyres are equal, bearing in mind that they may be a bit above those shown in the table. (The same applies to the two back tyres, but remember that their pressure should be different from the front).

If one tyre of a pair has a low pressure when hot, bring it up to the pressure of the other at the same end of the car; if they're both below the recommended cold pressure although warm, the safest thing to do is to bring them up to about 3 psi above it, to allow for cooling.

Topping up oil

Whenever you top up the oil level, always try to use the same grade and brand; and do avoid using cheap oil — the initial saving will probably be lost in increased engine wear over a prolonged period — or perhaps a short one!

When checking the oil level, ensure that the car's standing on level ground. Take out the dipstick, wipe it clean, then replace it fully. Pull it out again and note the oil level. Under no circumstances should the level be allowed to drop below the MIN mark. If the oil level is at this mark, about $\frac{7}{8}$ pint (0.5 litre) will be **21**

Checking a tyre pressure

Don't forget to check the spare tyre pressure

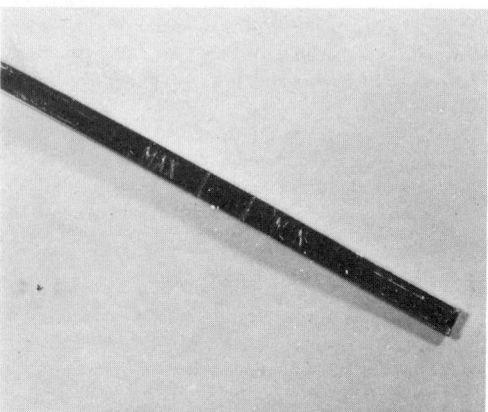

The oil level dipstick showing the maximum and minimum markings

Topping up the engine oil

Topping up the coolant level in the expansion tank

needed to bring it up to the 'MAX' mark. Avoid over-filling and wipe up any oil spilt.

Checking coolant level

If the engine's at its normal running temperature or higher, **take extra care** when removing the expansion tank filler cap. Place a rag over the cap, turn it slowly anti-clockwise to the first position and allow the pressure in the system to escape, then again turn anti-clockwise and remove carefully.

Grip the radiator top hose with both hands and squeeze to compress it, simultaneously noting the coolant movement within the expansion tank. The coolant level on releasing the hose should be adjacent to, or just below, the level marking arrow on the tank. Topping up will only be necessary if the level in the tank has fallen below half full.

If a considerable amount of water is required to top up or you're continually adding water during the winter months, the antifreeze mixture will be diluted and made less effective. So if antifreeze is in use, topping up should be done with water/antifreeze mixture in the correct proportions. In an emergency, though, plain water is better than nothing!

Self-service garages

Many garages now operate on a self-service basis so that the customer's subjected to the intricacies of refuelling his or her own vehicle. Regulars to this type of establishment need no introduction to its methods of operation and can usually be seen going through the routine at high speed like well-oiled robots. To the newcomer, the operation of the various kinds of pump can at first be confusing, but don't panic! Carefully read each instruction on the pump in turn before attempting to work it. When refuelling, insert the nozzle fully into the car's filler tube and try to regulate the fuel flow at an even rate so that it's not too fast. Most pumps now have an automatic anti flow-back valve fitted in them, which prevents any surplus petrol making a speedy exit from the filler neck all over the unsuspecting operator. On completion, don't forget to refit the petrol filler cap.

QUICK CHECK CHART

TYRE PRESSURES

Recommended pressures for cold tyres in lbf/in² (kgf/cm²)

Metro model	Front	Rear
998 cc models	32 (2.2)	28 (2.0)
1275 cc models (except automatic)	28 (2.0)	26 (1.8)
Automatic transmission models	30 (2.1)	26 (1.8)
Denovo 2 tyres (all models)	28 (2.0)	26 (1.8)

FUEL OCTANE RATING
All models

97 minimum (4-star)

FUEL TANK CAPACITY
All models

6.6 gallons (30 litres) approx

ENGINE OIL GRADE
All models

Multigrade SAE 15W/50

Fuel octane star rating symbols — use the correct grade for your model

In an Emergency

Servicing tasks and intervals have fortunately become fewer over the years, and consequently what was at one time a weekly 'rebuild' has become for many an optimistic motorist the annual chore, and this only because the MOT test is coming up! Small wonder then that the occasional spot of bother or breakdown still occurs, when the specified service checks and jobs are ignored, and this fact is even boasted about by many people.

This does not of course apply to everybody. A lot of owners religiously check, service and clean their car at regular intervals, and some almost wrap it up in the proverbial cotton wool each night.

However, even the most carefully looked-after car will let you down some day. Punctures are still a common event, and although changing a wheel isn't the major operation it used to be, it's still not a pastime to be recommended, especially as it always seems to need doing on a cold wet night; and you won't feel any better with your spouse or mother-in-law looking on in scorn as you discover that the spare's flat and you've no idea how the jack works. If you're not familiar with the jack supplied with your Metro, get acquainted with it – because one day you're going to need to use it!

Spares and repairs kit

The tool kit supplied with the car is the minimum necessary to change a wheel, and nothing more, so should a breakdown occur, you may well be thankful for a basic tool and spare parts kit of your own. Obviously it's not practical to motor around carrying vast quantities of spare parts and a full range of mechanic's tools, but a few of the items more likely to be needed, and easily used at the roadside, can get you out of a spot of bother. Apart from a selection of tools (these are discussed in *Tools for the Job)* the sort of things you should consider carrying are:

Spark plug – correctly gapped and clean

A length of HT lead sufficient to reach from the distributor to the furthest plug

Water pump/alternator drivebelt

Distributor rotor arm, set of points and condenser

Roll of insulating tape

A torch, or extension light and lead with crocodile clips

A container of spare coolant and a hose bandage

Fuses and spare light bulbs

Breakdown warning triangle

Tow-rope

Windscreen de-icer and scraper

Hand cleaner and rags

Your Haynes Handbook and/or Owner's Workshop **Manual**

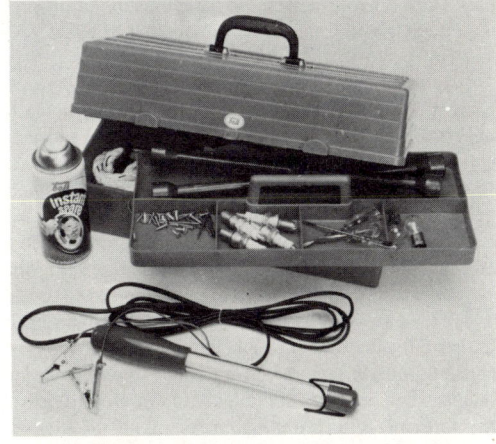

A box like this is useful for keeping your emergency repair kit together

An 'Instant Spare' aerosol in use on a flat tyre

If you want to carry emergency petrol, use an approved safety can of the type shown here. The detachable spout makes pouring easy, too

The list could of course be expanded indefinitely – for example, you might like to have a set of spare cooling system hoses instead of just a hose bandage. It's up to you to decide what you're likely to use in a roadside situation.

So far as the water pump/alternator drivebelt is concerned, it's worth mentioning that you can buy an emergency type which doesn't require any bolts to be loosened to fit it, and which will suit a wide variety of cars. With one of these in the car, you can get on your way quickly and fit a proper replacement belt at your leisure.

Another item well worth carrying is an aerosol can of ignition waterproofer, which is particularly beneficial on damp mornings and when motorway spray and rain get into your ignition system. If the car fails to start or misfires under these conditions, a quick squirt applied to the coil, ignition leads and distributor cap will chase off any moisture present and save much time and aggravation drying and cleaning the various individual components.

A further 'get you home' device worth carrying is an instant puncture repair in the form of an aerosol can. The nozzle is screwed on to the tyre valve, and releases sealant to seal the leak, together with gas to reinflate the tyre. It's suitable for tubed or tubeless tyres and will at the very least allow you to drive to a garage without getting your hands dirty.

Roadside breakdowns

If you break down or have to stop in an inconvenient spot such as a narrow road or just round a bend, pull over as far as possible to the left of the road and switch on your hazard warning lights. If you carry a warning triangle, place this in the road about 50 yards to the rear of your car facing the following traffic.

Where you're unable to repair the fault and have to walk for assistance, lock the car up and leave the sidelights on if dusk is falling.

If you have children or a dog with you, keep them under close control and don't let them run around and create an extra danger. Don't leave young children in an unattended car.

A breakdown on a motorway can be an alarming experience owing to the speed of other traffic. Pull the car on to the hard shoulder and switch on the hazard or sidelights. The 100-metre posts have arrows on them pointing the direction of the nearest emergency telephone which links you with the motorway police, who in turn will put you in touch with the AA or RAC if you're a member.

Return to your car as quickly as possible but keep well away from the carriageway. It may well be safer not to remain in the car while awaiting help, but in this case do get well away from the hard shoulder on to the verge or bank.

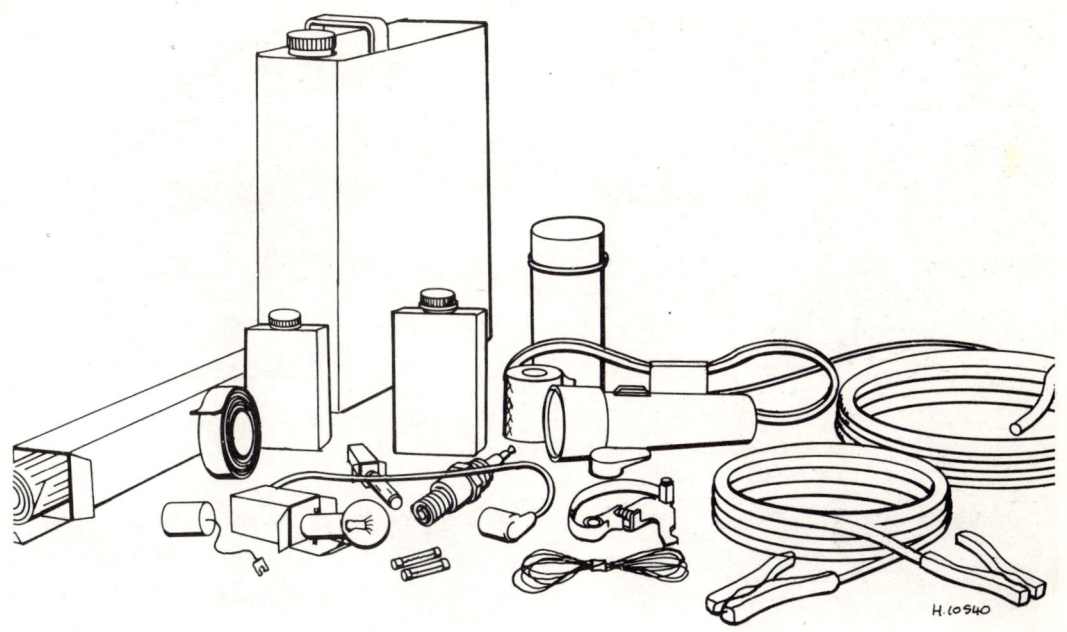

A few spares carried in the car can save you a long walk!

Jacking up and changing a wheel

Whenever the car's to be jacked up (either to change a wheel or for any other purpose) the car must be parked on firm, flat ground. The jack supplied with the vehicle is intended only for raising the car in the event of a puncture to change the wheel. It shouldn't be used to lift the car to perform any major tasks underneath unless it's further supported with chassis stands or blocks to make it secure.

Before jacking up, make sure the handbrake's firmly applied, engage first gear, and place blocks of some description each side of the wheel diagonally opposed to the one to be changed.

Use the special hub cover removal tool supplied with the car to prise free the cap, levering between the wheel and cap. Be prepared to catch the cap as it is released to avoid scratching it.

The wheel nuts are now accessible, and each nut should be loosened (anti-clockwise) about half a turn. If the nuts are reluctant to move under hand pressure, try using your foot on the spanner, but take care that it doesn't slip off the nut in the process.

Locate the jack so that it is under the jacking point adjacent to the wheel to be removed and engage the peg in the jack head into the hole in the jacking point. If the ground isn't too firm, put a piece of flat wood under the jack to provide additional support.

Having raised the jack, check that it's secure and the wheel chocks are still in position, then take off the wheel nuts and wheel.

Fit the spare wheel, and finger tighten the nuts (ensuring that their domed ends face the wheel), then lower and remove the jack. The wheel nuts must be fully tightened. Don't bend the spanner doing this – just make sure they're firmly tight but remember they'll have to come off again sometime! (It's not absolutely necessary, but advisable, to check the nuts for tightness later, after some miles have been covered). Finally, refit the hub plate and remove the chocks. Check the pressure in the replacement tyre as soon as possible, especially if it hasn't been checked recently. Don't forget to have the punctured tyre repaired or renewed at the earliest opportunity.

Denovo wheels and tyres – puncture procedure

On those models fitted with a set of Denovo wheels and tyres, puncture procedure is somewhat different, since the tyre is designed to be driven on at a limited speed and for a limited mileage in its deflated condition without damage. With minor punctures the Denovo tyre will either deflate and then partially reinflate to a lower than normal pressure, or reseal itself but with a drop in the normal tyre pressure. (This is why it is most important that the tyre pressures are checked on a weekly basis. Any sudden drop in pressure beyond 5 lbf/in^2 (0.35 **27**

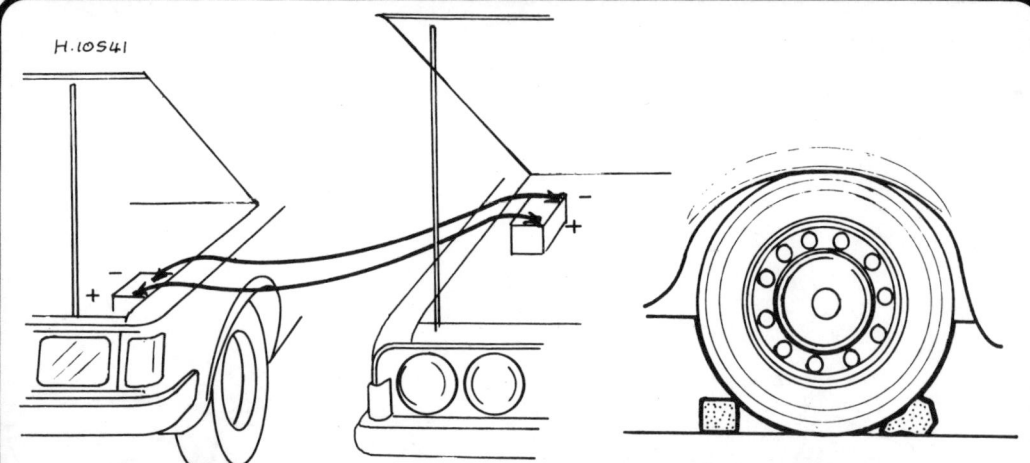

H.10541

Correct way to connect jump leads. Do not allow the car bodies to touch!

Always wedge the wheels before jacking up the car

Lever the hub cover (where fitted) free

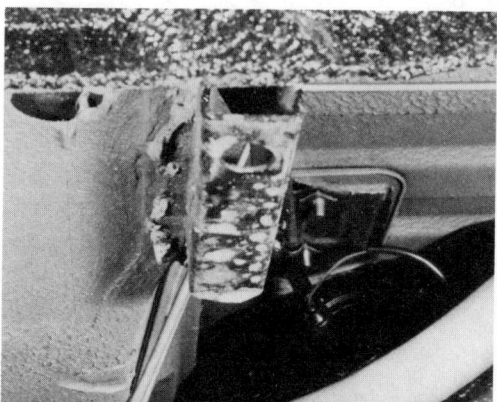

The jacking point showing the peg location hole

Jacking the car using the original jack

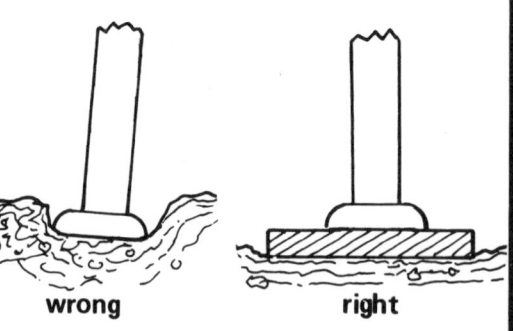

wrong   **right**

Spread the load under the foot of the jack

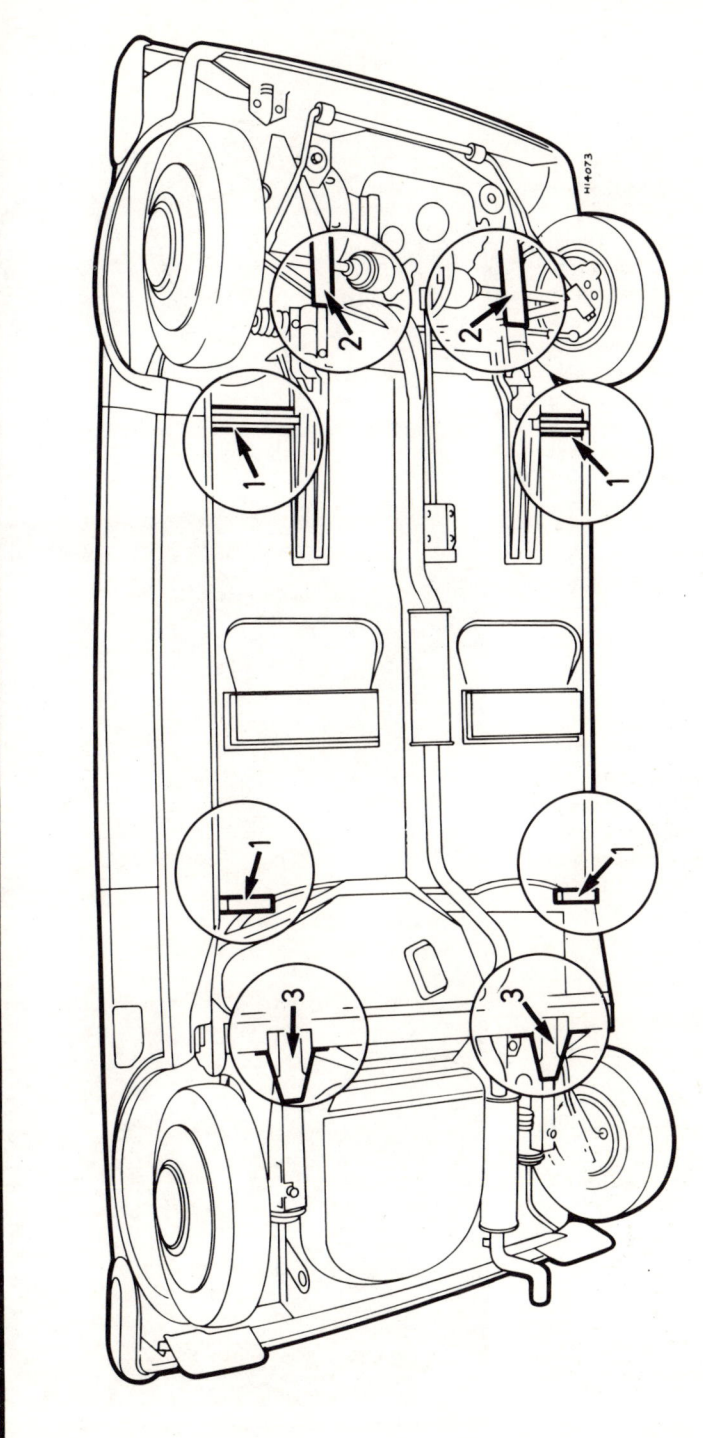

The jack support points under the Metro

1 Jacking brackets (use with original jack)
2 Front jacking points (servicing)
3 Rear jacking points (servicing)

kgf/cm²) necessitates the tyre being checked by a qualified Denovo dealer).

The tyre and wheel are designed to be run temporarily with the tyre partially deflated, but the speed must be kept down to a maximum of 50 mph (80 km/h) and the maximum distance a vehicle may be driven in this condition is 100 miles (160 km). To preserve the run-flat mileage, where a Denovo tyre dealer cannot be found locally, reinflate the tyre to its specified pressure to enable you to reach a Denovo specialist and have the repair made. A temporary repair kit is supplied with the car when new – most garages will have someone who knows how to use it.

In the event of the tyre blowing out, the damage to the tyre may be such that it will not partially reinflate. Even so, the car can still be driven at a reduced maximum speed of 40 mph (65 km/h) for a distance of 50 miles. Any mileage travelled with a flat tyre beyond the speed and distance specified could well damage the tyre case to the point where any repairs will be impossible.

When a puncture occurs when motoring, the first warnings that the driver has are poor handling and heavy steering, with possibly a noticeable change in the steering wheel angular position, a harsh vibrating ride and probably an audibly noisy one.

Maintenance of lights

Remember that a defective exterior light can be not only dangerous but also illegal. Carrying spare bulbs will enable you to replace blown ones as they occur. A failed interior lamp or panel bulb may be just a nuisance but an exterior lamp could be a life or death matter.

Headlamp bulb renewal
Metro, L and City models

With the bonnet open, pull the socket connector from the rear of the headlamp, and withdraw the rubber cover.

Release the clip and remove the headlamp bulb, but do not touch the bulb glass with fingers; if touched, clean it with methylated spirit.

Refitting is a reversal of removal, but make sure that the lug on the bulb flange engages with the notch on the reflector, and adjust the headlamp alignment as described below.

All other models

With the bonnet open, pull the rubber cover from the rear of the headlamp. Pull the socket connector from the bulb.

Release the clip and remove the headlamp bulb, but do not touch the bulb glass with the fingers; if

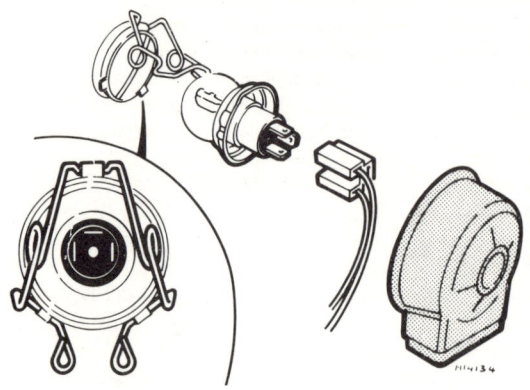

The headlamp bulb components for the Metro, L and City models

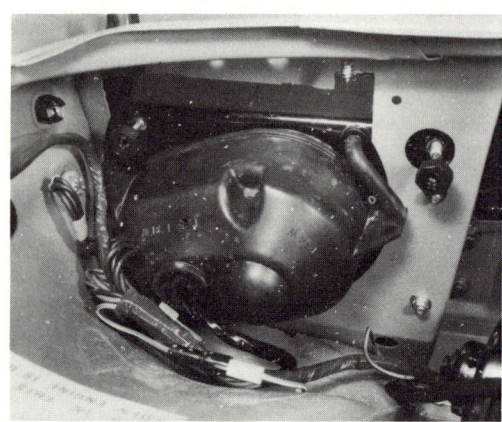

The headlamp rear cover (1.3 HLS)

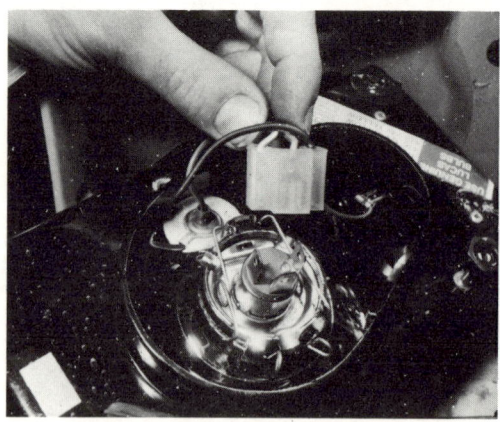

Removing the headlamp bulb connector (1.3 HLS)

touched, clean it with methylated spirit.

Refit in the reverse order, ensuring that the pip on the flange slots into the reflector location slots. The clip coils must rest on the base of the bulb and the clip legs fully engage under the reflector lugs. When reassembly is completed, reconnect the wiring and check for correct operation. Also check and if necessary adjust the headlamp alignment as given below.

Headlamp beam alignment

It is recommended that the alignment is carried out by a BL garage using modern beam setting equipment. However, in an emergency, the headlamp beam adjustments can be altered to provide an acceptable light pattern as described in *Service Scene*.

Sidelamps and front indicator lamp bulb renewal
Metro, L and City models

Remove the lens from the front bumper (2 screws). Push and twist the bulbs to remove them.

All other models

To remove the sidelamp bulb, pull back the rubber cover and pull out the bulb holder. Push and twist the bulb to remove it.

To remove the indicator bulb, pull back the rubber cover and turn the bulb holder anti-clockwise from the headlamp reflector. Push and twist the bulb to remove it.

Rear lamp cluster bulb renewal

Open the tailgate. Remove the two screws and the air vent. Remove the four screws and withdraw the lamp lens.

Push and twist the faulty bulb to remove it. Note that the stop/tail bulb has offset pins and can only be fitted in one position.

Rear number plate lamp bulb renewal

Press and twist the lamp lens to remove it. Push and twist the bulb to remove it.

Rear foglamp bulb renewal

Remove the two screws and withdraw the lens. Push and twist the bulb to remove it.

Note that the lens is tapered; the narrow end must face the side of the car.

Side repeater lamp bulb renewal

Reach up under the front wing, and pull the bulb holder from the lamp body. A wedge type bulb is fitted; pull it straight from the bulb holder.

When refitting the bulb holder, support the lamp body and lens from the outside. If the lamp body is displaced use adhesive to stick it to the wing.

Interior lamp bulb renewal

Prise the lamp from the roof, then depress the bulb and turn it through 90° to remove it. Do not trap the wires when refitting the lamp.

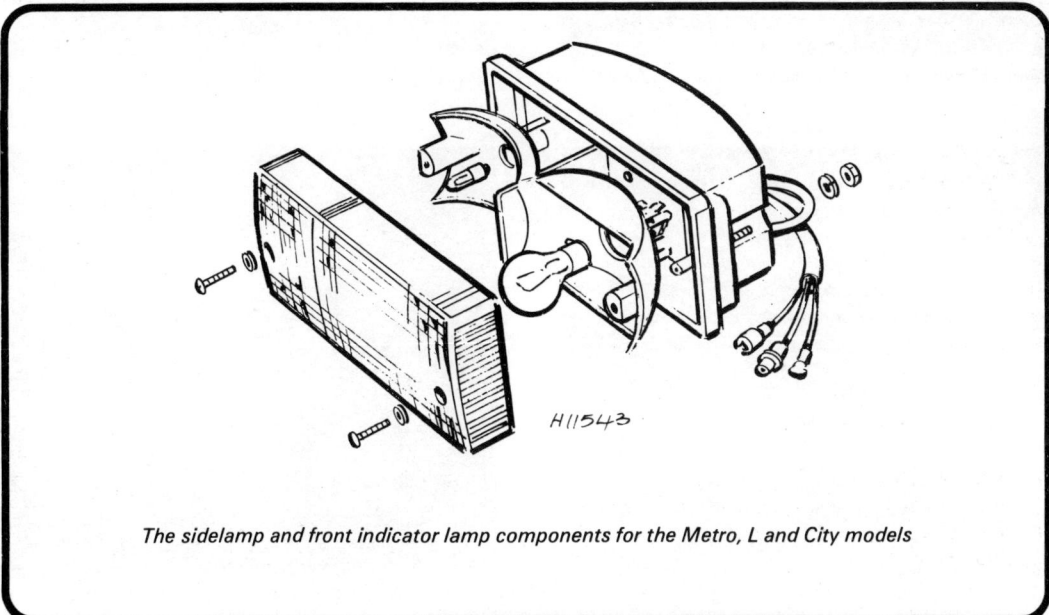

H11543

The sidelamp and front indicator lamp components for the Metro, L and City models

Withdrawing the headlamp bulb (1.3 HLS)

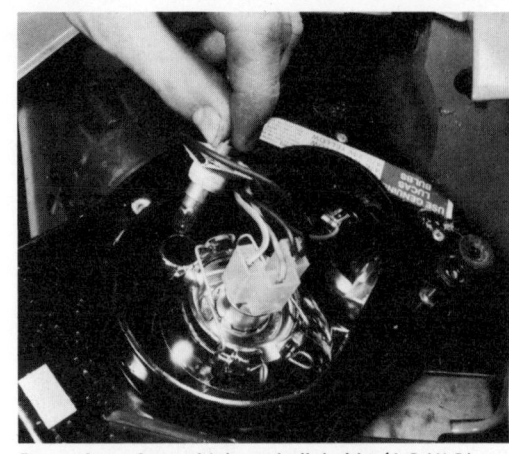

Removing a front sidelamp bulb holder (1.3 HLS)

Removing a front direction indicator bulb (1.3 HLS)

Removing the rear lamp cluster air vent

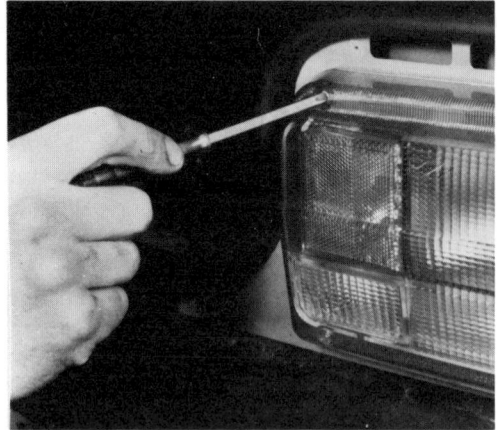

Remove the cluster unit lens retaining screws ...

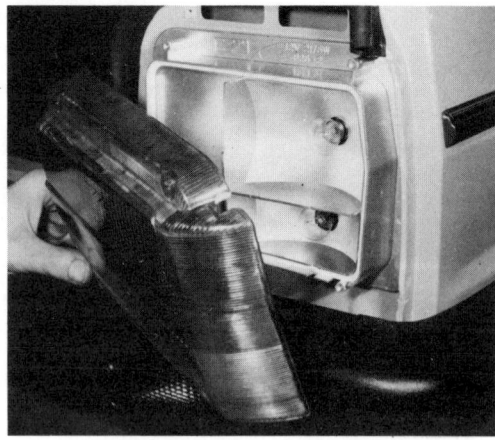

... and withdraw the lens for access to the bulbs

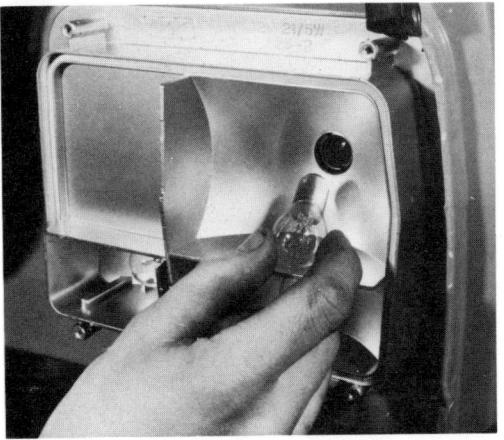

Removing a rear light bulb

The rear number plate lamp location

Removing the rear number plate lamp lens (lamp removed for clarity)

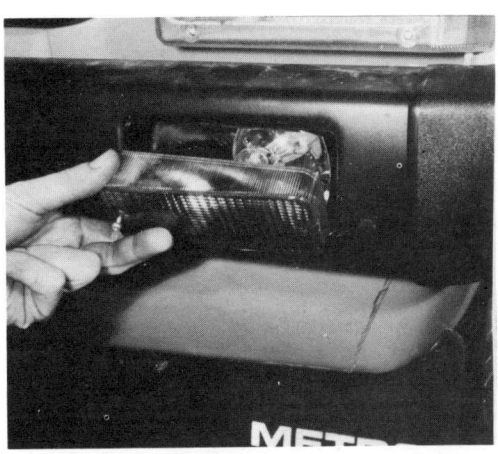

Removing the rear foglamp lens

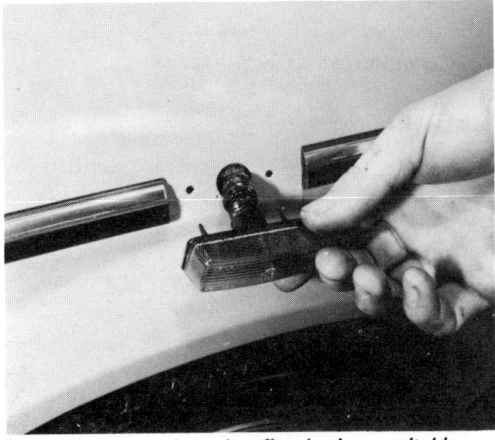

The side repeater lamp is refitted using a suitable adhesive to secure the main body in position

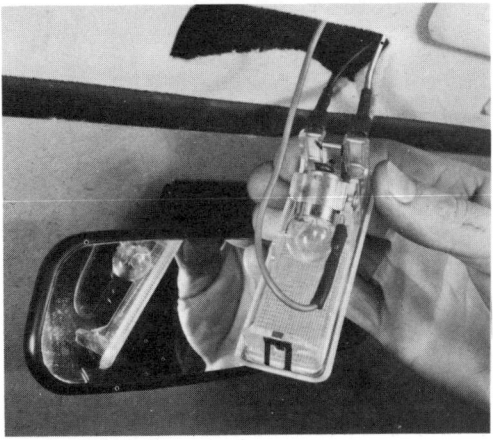

Interior light bulb removal

Fuses

The fuses are located behind the switch panel on the right-hand side of the dash panel. Access to them is gained by removing the two screws from the front of the switch panel, and pivoting the panel downwards.

The fuse locations are numbered together with the respective current rating, and the circuits protected are as follows:

Fuse 1 — *Direction indicators, stop lamps, reverse lamps, heated rear window and warning light*

Fuse 2 — *Interior lamp, hazard warning, lighter*

Fuse 3 — *Sidelamps, tail lamps, number plate lamps, panel lamps*

Fuse 4 — *Tailgate wiper motor, tailgate washer motor*

In addition to the main fuses, in-line fuses are provided to protect the following circuits:

Horn, rear foglamps, wiper motor, washer motor, heater motor

Always renew a fuse with one of identical rating, and never renew it more than once without finding the source of the trouble (usually a short-circuit). Never bypass persistently blowing fuses with silver foil or wire, or fit a fuse of a higher rating than that specified. Serious damage, or even fire, may result.

Towing and being towed

There may come the odd occasion when you need to tow something or be towed. Before you do, just stop and consider one or two things. To start with, if you want to tow, pick on something your own size or preferably smaller – remember you only have a Metro, not a Range Rover! The maximum permissible towing weights depend on the model, and are given in *Vital Statistics*.

Models fitted with automatic transmission should use the 'D' range when towing, except when descending steep hills when manual selection of 2nd or 3rd gear (manual hold) will provide engine braking. Note that 1st gear manual hold does not provide engine braking.

If it is your vehicle that is to be towed, ensure before starting that the ignition key is set at the 'I' or 'II' position and definitely **not** the 'O' position (whereby the steering will be locked!). Also check that the handbrake is fully released.

On automatic transmission models, do not tow unless the engine/transmission oil level is correct, select 'N' and restrict the towing speed to 30 mph (50 km/h). The maximum towing distance with this

Remove the switch panel retaining screws ...

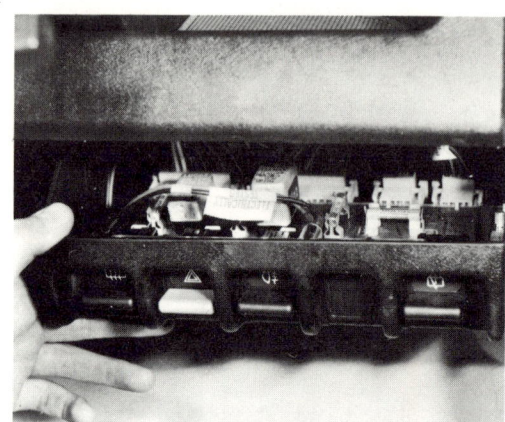

... then pivot the panel downwards ...

... for access to the fuses (also the warning/switch illumination bulb)

type of transmission must not exceed 30 miles (50 km). If the reason that you need to be towed is an excessively noisy or faulty transmission, your vehicle will have to be towed by a recovery vehicle able to suspend the front wheels clear of the ground to avoid the possibility of causing further damage to the **transmission.**

Do not attach a tow-rope to the rear lashing eye

Whatever model you have, remember to use a good quality tow-rope/chain in sound condition. When attaching it, be most careful about choosing

the attachment point, and ensure that it's not fixed to a suspension or steering component. Try to attach it centrally to a sound part of the sub-frame. The distance between the two vehicles must be limited to 15 feet. If the rope's too short, the driver in the towed car is in for a nerve-racking experience!. **Do not** use the rear lashing eye on the Metro for towing.

Hang a notice clearly in the rear window of the towed vehicle to warn following motorists that you're 'On Tow'.

Take up any slack in the rope gently, and once under way endeavour to keep the rope taut. Sudden jerking on the rope by the towing car may cause the rope to break or damage one of the vehicles. Being towed is a tedious pastime, especially over long distances, so keep alert at all times or you may end up with two cars on tow!

It should also be remembered on models fitted with servo-assisted brakes that without the engine running, the power assistance for the brakes won't be available, so harder foot pressure will be necessary when braking.

If you're having trouble starting the engine of an automatic and had thought about getting a push or a tow to start, don't waste your time — it won't work. The only solution if the battery's flat is to connect up a charged battery in parallel using 'jump leads'. Make sure that you connect positive to positive and vice-versa, and connect to the charged battery first.

Save it!

Despite the reliability of modern cars, the continuous increase in power output combined with more miles per gallon, and the greater mileages between the necessary servicing procedures, motoring costs are still relatively high. This is mainly due to high production costs and regular increases in the price of fuel. Because of this, motoring to most people has to be achieved on a fairly tight budget, and it therefore follows that running costs should be carefully analysed and wherever possible, savings made. In this Chapter we cover several points which should help to reduce your daily motoring costs – or at least prevent them from increasing quite as fast as they might otherwise do, but at the same time without reducing the safety of your car.

Maintenance and driving habits

Your Metro is potentially one of the most economical cars on the road – provided it's properly maintained! Whether you do the servicing yourself or take the car to a BL dealer, the aim is the same – to enable the car to run efficiently and safely. Don't skimp on servicing or postpone a major service, it's false economy.

With the engine in a good state of tune, the rest is up to you. Don't race away from every set of traffic lights, or scream up the motorway with your right foot on the floor. You'll pay for such behaviour at the petrol pump in the short term, and maybe in frequent tyre and repair bills in the longer term! This is not to say that you should drive everywhere at 40 mph, but try exercising a little restraint in your use of the throttle. You can save a lot of fuel, and avoid wear and tear, without increasing your journey times very much.

Town driving is notoriously uneconomical. Try to avoid rush hour traffic, and switch off your engine if the queue you're in looks like being stationary for half a minute or more. In lighter traffic, try to maintain a steady progess rather than alternating between full throttle and heavy braking. Remember also that the engine uses most fuel (and suffers most wear) in the first mile or so after a cold start. If your motoring consists largely of short journeys, you're never going to achieve the economy possible on the open road.

Economy devices

If we could believe everything published about economy devices, we'd be able to fit the lot and end up with a car that would save more fuel than it used! Obviously this isn't going to happen, and the evidence produced by the motoring magazines doesn't lend much weight to the various manufacturers' arguments. If you're considering fitting any of these items (which range from manifold modifiers to spark boosters and fuel pressure regulators), it can only be assumed that your car isn't giving you the miles per gallon you originally expected when you bought it. Before you lash out with your hard earned cash, first check that the engine's in good condition and that the necessary adjustments have been made correctly.

If you've recently had your engine reconditioned and are positive that it's adjusted correctly, and yet you still get poor consumption figures, it may be that the carburettor's badly worn or damaged. Your money would therefore be far better spent on having the existing carburettor checked and reconditioned by a carburettor specialist or Leyland dealer than on a dubious gadget.

The distributor and coil are likely trouble spots for poor economy. To get a complete check and diagnosis, take your car to a tuning specialist who has the necessary knowledge, and perhaps electronic diagnosis equipment, to pinpoint a trouble spot in a relatively short time, and you'll soon recover your outlay in cheaper running costs.

One 'economy device' (to use the term in its widest sense) which *can* repay its cost quite quickly is a vacuum or engine performance gauge, such as the 'Milemiser' from Smiths Industries. This enables a constant check to be kept on the engine's operating range and the idea is to keep the needle in the 'good' sector as much as possible – indicating optimum efficiency and therefore minimum fuel consumption. One of these devices will quickly reveal just how important your own right foot is in the fuel economy game!

Smiths 'Milemiser', a useful aid to economical driving

The luxurious Vanden Plas version of the Metro is available with a trip computer. This useful optional extra is designed to provide the motorist with trip mileage, time and fuel consumption data. Where such a device is fitted the driver has a real advantage in being able to adjust his driving habits to suit conditions whilst obtaining the best possible fuel economy from the vehicle, but only providing it is kept in a good state of tune! The operational details of this device are given in *In the Driving Seat*.

Fuel

Your car's designed to run on a particular grade of fuel (star rating). Don't buy fuel that's of a higher rating than this, because you're wasting your money. On the other hand, if you buy a lower rating fuel your engine performance (and probably your engine too) will suffer. If you *are* forced to buy inferior fuel, drive carefully until you can get the correct grade; in these circumstances it's also beneficial to retard the ignition by a couple of degrees, but you've got the bother of resetting it again later.

Lubricants and the like

Good cheap engine oils are available, but because it's so difficult to find out which cheap ones *are* good, it's safest to stay clear of them. There are plenty of good multigrade engine oils on the market and quite a few are available at sensible prices from supermarkets and the DIY motoring and accessory shops.

Unless circumstances should force you to, don't buy oil in pint or half-litre cans. This is the most expensive way of buying, particularly if it's from a filling station. The 5-litre (they used to be one gallon) cans are adequate for most purposes, and contain just about the right amount for an engine oil change; an extra can for topping-up between oil changes will probably be required, particularly if your pride and joy happens to be a bit of an oil burner.

Oil is also available in larger drums (which can be fitted with a tap) sometimes at an even bigger price saving. A telephone call or visit to nearby wholsesalers may well prove worthwhile.

Antifreeze is always cheaper if you go to the motoring shops, but bulk buying doesn't normally apply because you never need to buy in any real quantity.

As for greases, brake fluid, etc, you'll save a little at the motoring shops but again you'll never need large quantities — just make sure that you buy something that's a good quality.

Additives

Oil and fuel additives have been with us for a long time and no doubt will be around for many years to come. It's pretty unlikely that there are any bad additives around, but there's not a great deal of evidence to suggest that there are many good ones. The major oil manufacturers will tell you that their oils are adequate on their own, in which case you'll only need additives if the oil you're using isn't much good. A fuel additive of the upper cylinder lubricant type is generally accepted as a good thing, one of its main functions being to prevent carbon building up around the piston rings and ring grooves, which means that the piston rings can seal more effectively. The way in which a car is used, whether it is just a runabout which never gets really warm or spends most of its life on long runs, has a far greater influence than additives in determining engine life.

Insurance

Like some of the other things that we've discussed, the service you're going to get from your insurance company will be related to the cost of the cover obtained. A cheap policy's good until you need to make a claim, and then the sort of snags you're going to come across are 'How do I get hold of an accessor to inspect the damage?', or 'How will it affect my No Claim Bonus?'

There are one or two legitimate ways of reducing the policy premium, perhaps by insuring for 'owner driver only', 'two named drivers', or an agreement to pay an agreed amount (excess) of any claim. Many large companies have a discount scheme for their employees if they use the same insurance company; this also applies to bank and Civil Service employees. You may also get a better bargain by insuring through one of the Motoring Associations if you're a member. **37**

What it all adds up to is: (1) Insure well; (2) See what you can get in the way of discounts; and (3) Find out exactly what you're covered for.

Tyres

As you may know, Metros are fitted with radial ply tyres as standard equipment. Although radial tyres aren't cheap, they're definitely superior to the crossply tyre in both roadholding and wear potential. Don't be tempted to fit crossply tyres to your Metro as a means of saving a few pounds — the handling of the car will probably be very poor if you do fit them. When purchasing tyres, try to shop around, you've probably got a few tyre specialists in your area who give good discounts and free fitting service; and remember that your local garage or BL dealer may be the most expensive place to buy new tyres.

Obviously it's best to purchase one of the well known brands of tyre, but in recent years quite a few names have appeared on the scene, some of which can offer favourable price reductions. If you're considering buying tyres of a lesser known brand name, try to first acquire some independent information as to their safety and reliability.

Many suppliers give fair discounts on their tyres; some, on presentation of membership cards of certain clubs and organisations, will reduce their price even more.

If your vehicle is fitted with a set of Denovo wheels and tyres, you will have no option but to renew them with identical replacements as they are of a special design. With this type of tyre you should check the pressures weekly without fail, since any drop in pressure in excess of 5 lbf/in^2 (0.35 kgf/cm^2) will necessitate inspection and possible repair by a qualified Denovo dealer. Failure to do this could lead to serious damage to the tyre and the need to renew it prematurely. Such neglect could therefore prove expensive!

Now let's just briefly consider how to make tyres last. First, keep them inflated properly (see *Filling Station Facts* for the correct pressures). Second, drive sensibly (ie no race-track starts or cornering). Third, make sure the wheels are balanced properly (a job for a garage or tyre specialist).

Batteries

Next to tyres, batteries are the most commonly found parts sold by specialists. A top quality battery may cost up to three times the price of the cheapest one that'll fit your car.

Once again, price is related to quality, but isn't necessarily directly proportional. A battery with a twelve month guarantee ought to last that long and a little bit more, but batteries always seem to fail at

embarrassing or inconvenient times so it's worthwhile getting something a little bit better. Many of the accessory shops and tyre dealers sell good quality batteries with two or three year guarantees. Buy one of these — it'll be worthwhile in the long run and still cost quite a bit less than the dearest ones around. And if you look after it, it'll look after you, too.

By the way, before you lash out on a new battery, make sure that it's really a battery that you need — you'll feel pretty stupid if the trouble turns out to have been in the charging system!

Exhaust systems

The average car gets through several exhaust systems in the course of its life, the actual number depending on the sort of journeys for which the car's used (lots of short journeys will mean condensation remaining inside the exhaust system and helping it to rust out more quickly).

The best place to go when your Metro needs a replacement exhaust (or maybe just part of the system) is one of the specialist 'exhaust centres' which have sprung up in recent years. They keep huge stocks to fit most mass-produced cars, and offer free fitting as well as discount prices on the parts themselves. You'll almost certainly show a worthwhile saving compared with getting your BL dealer to fit the exhaust (which will involve labour charges as well!).

If you're planning to keep your car for several years it would certainly be worth thinking about an exhaust system made from stainless steel. It'll normally cost you considerably more than an ordinary mild steel replacement, but on the other hand should last the remainder of the car's life. If you're interested, talk it over with one of the exhaust specialists — they're usually stockists of the stainless steel kind too.

Roof racks

The ever-faithful roof rack has proved a boon to so many motorists, for the extra holiday luggage, but how often do you see cars being driven around with an empty roof rack still attached? Many estimates have been made of the increase in fuel consumption caused by a roof rack, due to wind resistance, and the generally accepted figure is around 10%; with a loaded rack, this figure can be as high as 30%. The moral, then, is obvious; don't use a roof rack unless you have to, and always remove it when it's not in use.

Buying spare parts

Apart from the oils and greases which you're going to need, it won't be long before you have to buy a few bits and pieces to keep things running smoothly. Please *do* remember to clean up any parts which are traded in on an exchange basis (eg brake shoes) and wherever possible, check that any replacement parts look the same as the old one, either by direct comparison, if this can be done, or by reference to any of the illustrations in the appropriate section of this book.

Spare parts and accessories are available from many sources, but the following should act as a good guide when they're required:

Officially appointed garages

Although BL dealers should be able to supply just about everything for your car, it's generally true to say that the prices may be higher than you might pay for 'pattern' parts. However, buy only 'BL' genuine parts if your car is still under warranty.

Other garages

In recent years the big British car manufacturers have introduced a replacement parts scheme whereby they market parts for each other's cars under trade names such as Mopar, Unipart and Motorcraft. Though you'll pay the same sort of prices for any of these parts ranges, you may well find that your local Talbot or Ford dealer can supply you with guaranteed parts for your Metro and that can't be a bad thing.

Accessory shops

These are usually the best places to get items like contact breaker points, oil filters, brake shoes and pads, spark plugs, light bulbs, fanbelts, lubricants, touch-up paints etc – the very things you're going to need for the general servicing of the car. They also sell general accessories and charge lower prices but, what's equally important, they have convenient opening hours and can often be found not too far from home.

Motor factors

Good factors will stock all the more important components of the engine, gearbox, suspension and braking systems, and often provide guaranteed parts on an exchange basis. They're particularly useful to the more advanced do-it-yourself motorist.

Vehicle identification numbers

Before undertaking any service or repair tasks on your Metro we recommend that you read through the relevant instructions to see just what's involved and what parts are likely to need replacing.

If you know in advance which items are to be renewed, they can be bought or ordered beforehand

Vehicle identification plate

Engine number location

and thus save time and trouble. It may be of course that the offending assembly will have to be dismantled before you can decide which parts need to be renewed.

Whatever the case, when ordering spare parts, it's always helpful and sometimes essential that the vehicle identification numbers (engine number and chassis number) are quoted. You may have intended to make a note of these before but not got around to it – if this is the case, note that now – in your diary perhaps, or inside the cover of this Handbook.

The *vehicle identification number* is stamped on a plate on the left-hand side of the bonnet lock crossmember.

The *engine number* is stamped on a plate attached to the front of the cylinder block by the alternator upper mounting.

Vital Statistics

Note: *Full specifications for MG and Vanden Plas models were not available at the time of writing. Those items known to differ from the other models in the Metro range have been listed below. If in doubt, contact your BL dealer.*

ENGINE
Type

4-stroke, 4-cylinder in-line, overhead valve, transversely mounted

Identification code

998 cc	99H
1275 cc	12H

General specifications

	99H	**12H**
Bore	2.54 in (64.59 mm)	2.78 in (70.61 mm)
Stroke	3.00 in (76.20 mm)	3.20 in (81.28 mm)
Capacity	60.96 cu in (998 cc)	77.80 cu in (1275 cc)
Firing order	1-3-4-2 (No 1 cylinder at pulley end)	

Compression ratio:

998cc low compression (fleet option)	8.3:1
998 cc (standard)	9.6:1
998 cc (HLE)	10.3:1
1275 cc (except MG)	9.4:1
1275 cc (MG)	10.5:1

Valve clearances (cold)

All models except MG	0.012 in (0.30 mm) inlet and exhaust
MG models:	
Inlet	0.012 in (0.30 mm)
Exhaust	0.015 in (0.38 mm)

Lubrication system

Oil pump type	Bi-rotor
System pressure:	
Idling	15 lbf/in^2 (1.05 kgf/cm^2)
Running	60 lbf/in^2 (4.2 kgf/cm^2)
Warning light operating pressure	6 to 10 lbf/in^2 (0.4 to 0.7 kgf/cm^2)
Oil capacity, including filter:	
Manual transmission	8.5 pints (4.8 litres)
Automatic transmission	8.75 pints (5.0 litres)

COOLING SYSTEM

System type

Thermo-system, pressurised, belt-driven pump. Front-mounted radiator and electric cooling fan

40 *System capacity*

8.5 pints (4.8 litres) including heater

Cutaway view of a Metro

VITAL STATISTICS

Thermostat opening temperature   88°C (190°F)

Drivebelt tension   0.16 in (4 mm) deflection under firm thumb pressure between water pump and alternator pulleys

FUEL SYSTEM
System type
Rear-mounted fuel tank, mechanical diaphragm pump, SU carburettor

Carburettor type
998 cc models	SU HIF 38
1275 cc models	SU HIF 44

Idle speed
All 998 cc models (except later HLE – see below)	750 rpm
HLE models from engine No 99H 962P 148301	650 rpm
All 1275 cc models (except MG)	750 rpm
MG models	850 rpm

Fast idle speed
998cc models (except later HLE)	1300 rpm
1275 cc and later HLE models	1100 rpm

IGNITION SYSTEM
System type
12 volt, contact breaker and coil, distributor with self-cleaning points

Coil
Make and type	Lucas 16C6 or AC Delco 9977230
Ballast resistor	1.3 to 1.5 ohms

Distributor
Make and type	Lucas 45D4 or 59D4, or Ducellier
Direction of rotation	Anti-clockwise
Contact breaker gap	0.014 to 0.016 in (0.35 to 0.40 mm)
Dwell angle:	
All except later HLE models	$57° \pm 5°$
HLE models from engine No 99H 962P 148301	$54° \pm 5°$

Ignition timing*
998 cc models (except HLE)	15° BTDC
HLE models:	
Up to engine No 99H 962P 148300	$8° \pm 2°$ BTDC
From engine No 99H 962P 148301	$7°\,^{+0°}_{-2°}$ BTDC
1275 cc models	11° BTDC

*At 1500 rpm, vacuum disconnected

Spark plugs
Make and type	Unipart GSP 263, Champion RN9Y, or equivalent
Electrode gap	0.025 in (0.64 mm)

CLUTCH
Clutch type Single dry plate and diaphragm spring; hydraulic actuation

Release lever clearance (where applicable) 0.04 in (1 mm)

MANUAL GEARBOX
Gearbox type Four forward speeds, one reverse; synchromesh on all forward gears

Gear ratios	**Early models**	**Later models**
1st	3.53:1	3.647:1
2nd	2.22:1	2.185:1
3rd	1.43:1	1.425:1
4th	1.00:1	1.00:1
Reverse	3.54:1	3.667:1

Lubrication Common with engine oil

AUTOMATIC TRANSMISSION
Type AP four-speed with manual hold/change facility

Gear ratios	
1st	2.690:1
2nd	1.845:1
3rd	1.460:1
4th	1.000:1
Reverse	2.690:1

Lubrication Common with engine oil

FINAL DRIVE
Ratio

998 cc models (except HLE)	3.647:1
1275 cc models (except automatic) and HLE	3.444:1
Automatic models	2.760:1

DRIVESHAFTS
Type Solid shafts, splined to inner and outer constant velocity joints

BRAKES
System type Discs front, drums rear. Dual hydraulic circuit, servo-assisted on 1.3 models. Cable-operated handbrake to rear wheels

Disc brakes

Disc diameter	8.35 in (213 mm)
Disc thickness	0.37 in (9.6 mm)
Pad lining minimum thickness	0.125 in (3 mm)

Drum brakes

Drum internal diameter	7.0 in (177.9 mm)
Shoe lining minimum thickness	0.0625 in (1.6 mm)

ELECTRICAL SYSTEM

System type	12 volt, negative earth

Battery

Type	Lead acid
Capacity (typical)	30 to 40 Ah

Alternator

Make and type	Lucas 18 ACR or Motorola 9AR 2683G
Output	43 to 45 amps

Starter motor

Make and type	Lucas M35J (inertia) or M35JPE (pre-engaged)

Fuses	**Circuits protected**
No 1 (17 amps)*	Direction indicators, stop lamps, reversing lamps, heated rear window
No 2 (12 amps)*	Interior lamp, hazard warning system, cigarette lighter
No 3 (8 amps)*	Sidelamps, tail lamps, number plate lamp, panel lamps
No 4 (8 amps)*	Tailgate wiper and washer
Line fuses	Horn, rear foglamps, wiper, washer and heater motors

Fuse ratings are for continuous current, 'Blow' ratings are approximately double

Bulbs (typical)	**Wattage**
Headlamps (base models)	45/40
Headlamps (other models)	60/50
Sidelamps	4
Direction indicators, reversing lamps, rear foglamps	21
Side repeater lamps	5
Stop and tail lamps	5/21
Number plate lamp	6
Interior lamp	10
Switch illumination lamps	0.75
Instrument panel lamps	1.2
Ignition (no-charge) warning lamp	2

SUSPENSION AND STEERING

Suspension type

Front	Independent, Hydragas spring units, telescopic shock absorbers, anti-roll bar
Rear	Independent. Trailing arm operating interconnected Hydragas spring units

Steering

Type	Rack-and-pinion, flexible coupling
Turns lock-to-lock	3.3

Front wheel alignment

Toe-out	0 to 0.125 in (0 to 3 mm)
Camber angle	0° ± 30'
Caster angle	2° 06' position ± 1°

Rear wheel alignment

Toe	0° 30' toe-in to 0° 30' toe-out
Camber angle	1° negative ± 30'

Wheels

Type:

All except MG models	Pressed steel disc
MG models	Alloy

Size:

Steel (except Denovo)	4.50B x 12
Denovo	95 x 320
Alloy	5.0 x 12

Tyres

Size:

998 cc models (except Denovo)	135SR x 12 or 155/70R x 12
1275 cc models (except Denovo and MG)	155/70R x 12
Denovo	160/65R x 320
MG models	155/70SR x 12
Pressures	See *Quick-Check Chart*

GENERAL DIMENSIONS AND WEIGHTS

Dimensions

Turning circle (approx)	33 ft 6 in (10.2 m)
Wheelbase	88.6 in (2.25 m)
Overall length	134.1 in (3.405 m)
Overall width	60.9 in (1.546 m)
Overall height	53.5 in (1.360 m)
Ground clearance	4.4 to 6.5 in (112 to 165 mm) according to model

Weights

Kerb weights (with full fuel tank):

Metro Standard	1620 lb (735 kg)
Metro L	1638 lb (743 kg)
Metro HLE	1646 lb (747 kg)
Metro 1.3 S	1662 lb (754 kg)
Metro 1.3 L and HLS	1695 b (769 kg)
Metro Automatic	1766 lb (804 kg)
MG Metro	1785 lb (811 kg)

Maximum towing weight:

998 cc models (except HLE)	1874 lb (850 kg)
HLE	1433 lb (650 kg)
1275 cc models	2094 lb (950 kg)
Maximum payload	705 lb (320 kg)
Maximum roof rack load	106 lb (48 kg)

Tools for the Job

For anyone intending to tackle car servicing, a selection of good down-to-earth tools is a basic requirement. The initial outlay, even though it may appear to be something approaching the national defence budget, could well be less than the labour charges for one full service; on top of this, you should be paying less for the oil and replacement parts by getting them yourself so, provided you've two or three hours to spare, you must be on to a winner.

The tools supplied with the vehicle when new enable the owner to change a roadwheel, and that's about all. It is therefore advisable to obtain at least a basic tool kit for carrying in the vehicle in order to be able to cope with minor adjustment and possibly breakdowns. This 'basic' kit should comprise two screwdrivers (one cross-headed), a pair of pliers, a small or medium adjustable spanner, a spark plug spanner and a set of feeler gauges. As both metric and Imperial (UNF) thread fittings are used on the Metro, a set of suitable combination spanners to cover the more common sizes should also be made up and carried. These items will be the basic essential requirements needed.

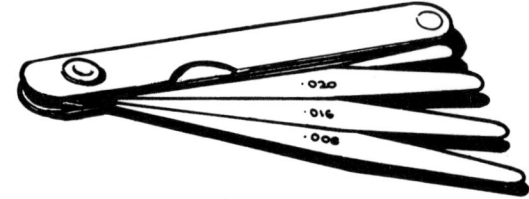

Feeler gauges

A small but important point when buying tools is the quality. You don't have to buy the very best in the shop but, on the other hand, the cheapest probably aren't much good. Have a word with the manager or proprietor if you're in doubt; he'll tell you what's good value for money.

If you intend to do the routine service and maintenance tasks on your Metro as well, additional tools will be required. It's very difficult to tell you exactly what you're going to need, but the list below should be a help in building up a good tool kit.

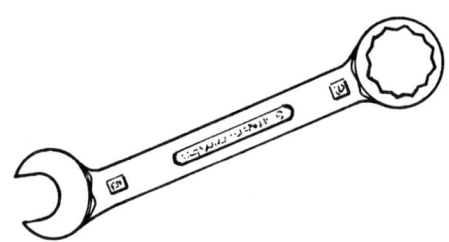

Combination ring/flat spanner

Combination spanners – $\frac{7}{16}$ to $\frac{15}{16}$ in AF, 10 to 17 mm metric
Adjustable spanner – 9 inch
Spark plug spanner (with rubber insert)
Engineer's hammer
Spark plug gap adjustment tool
Set of feeler gauges
Brake adjuster spanner

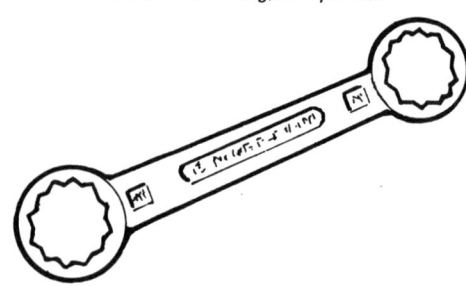

Double-ended ring spanner

Screwdriver – 4 in x $\frac{1}{4}$ in dia (plain)
Screwdriver – 4 in blade x $\frac{1}{4}$ in dia (crosshead)
Pliers – 6 inch
Junior hacksaw
Tyre pump
Tyre pressure gauge
Grease gun
Oil can
Fine emery cloth or oilstone
Wire brush (small)
Funnel (medium size)
Hydraulic jack or strong screw type
Pair of axle stands (concrete or wooden blocks will do if you're careful about choosing them)
Hose brush

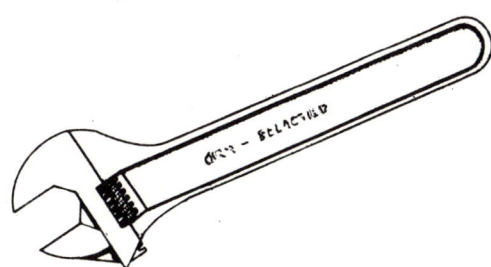

Adjustable spanner

Additionally you'll need suitable containers to drain the engine, gearbox and axle oils into, and also one that can be used to wash parts in. An old 1 gallon oil can will do to drain the oil into if you cut a suitable size hole in the side face. An old washing-up bowl's ideal too, and can also be used to clean components in – but husbands – check with your wife first, she may not have bought a replacement and you don't want any more expense at the moment! Some non-fluffy rags will also be required to clean parts with and to mop-up the odd drop of oil spilt. If sawdust's available, keep some handy to soak up any major oil spillage. If you can buy, beg or borrow a boiler suit to work in, this will help to keep you clean and allows greater freedom of movement when working underneath the car.

You will find that a pair of metal ramps is a very useful investment, providing an alternative to the jack or axle stands when you want to get at the underside of the car but don't need to remove the wheel(s). Most ramps available give a lift of between 9 inches and 1 ft and you can, of course, drive either the front or back end of the car on to them – but you'll still need to engage a gear and chock the other two wheels for safety's sake.

Hopefully, your attempts at car servicing are going to show you that it can all be worthwhile, and having worked your way through the various jobs listed in the Service Schedules you'll be able to see that there are many others which can be done without becoming a mechanical wizard. For this purpose, Haynes publish a first class Owner's Workshop Manual for the Metro models which details just about every operation that can conceivably be done on these cars. It'll mean buying a few more tools, but to hell with it – you're out to save yourself some money and get a job done in the process.

If and when you do get to this stage, the next items to put on your tool kit shopping list are a good

Axle stand

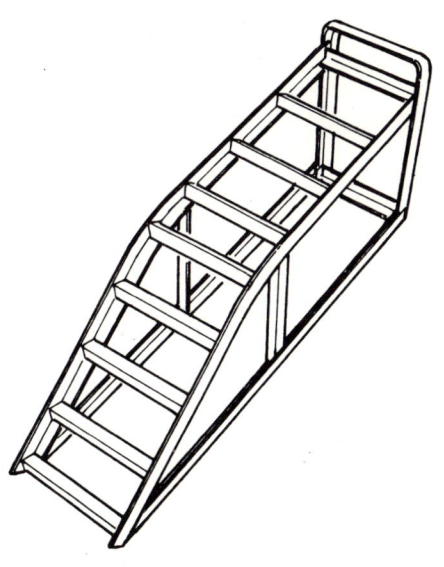

Steel ramp

socket spanner set ($\frac{1}{2}$ inch drive, and preferably including a ratchet, extension bar, universal joint and spark plug socket) and a torque wrench for use with the sockets.

While we're talking about tools, it's worth mentioning some of the tune-up aids that are on the market. A visit to a good motor accessory shop can be an enlightening experience, just to show you the sort of things available. Later in this book, you'll find a bit about 'bolt-on goodies', but all we'll concern ourselves with here are three items.

Stroboscopic timing lamp: The most accurate way of checking your ignition timing (that's the time at which the spark occurs) is with the engine running, and for this a stroboscopic (strobe) light is used. This is connected to No 1 spark plug lead and the beam is shone on to the timing marks. Any proprietary light is supplied with full connecting and operating instructions.

Dwell angle meter: This is used for measuring the period of time for which the distributor points remain closed during the ignition cycle of one cylinder, and provides a more accurate method of setting-up the ignition than can be done by simply setting the points gap. Dwell angle meters sometimes incorporate a tachometer (rev counter if you prefer), which can be useful for checking engine idle speed.

Cylinder compression gauge: This is very useful for tracing the cause of a fall-off in engine performance. It consists of a pressure gauge and non-return valve, and is simply screwed into a spark plug hole while the engine is turned over on the starter.

Two other useful items are a hydrometer, which is used for checking the specific gravity of the battery electrolyte (this will tell you if you have a dud cell which won't hold a charge), and a 12-volt lamp on an extension lead with crocodile clips which can be connected to the battery terminals.

Care of your tools

Having bought a reasonable set of tools and equipment, it's the easiest thing in the world to abuse them. After use, always wipe off any dirt and grease using a clean, dry cloth before putting them away. Never leave them lying around after they've been used. A simple rack on the garage wall, for things you don't need to carry in the car, is a good idea.

Keep all your spanners and the like in a metal box – you can wrap some rags around them to stop them rattling if you're going to carry them in the car. Any gauges and meters should be carefully put away so that they don't get damaged or rusty. Do take a little care over maintaining your tools too. Screwdriver blades, for example, inevitably lose their keen edges, and a little timely attention with a file won't go amiss.

Service Scene

The mere mention of the words 'service' or 'maintenance' to some people will make them cringe as they visualise technical obstacles and problems. This attitude is usually tempered with two other main excuses for avoiding the issue, these being (a) the amount of time the servicing procedures might take, and (b) the thought of getting dirty. Well, there was a time (there still is with some vehicles) when such reasoning was valid, but not with the Metro. Most items are easily accessible and no specialised tools or knowledge are required to service it.

Whilst it has to be agreed that one can expect to get at least a pair of hands dirty when servicing, these can easily be washed on completion! If you consider the savings to be made in hard-earned cash compared with having a garage do the jobs needed, you will find such small sacrifices well worthwhile.

Some people may ask 'why service the car at all? If it's running alright, leave it alone'. This is an attitude inviting disaster. Servicing and inspection of the vehicle's main components at regular intervals is necessary to keep the car safe, to prolong its active life, and to maintain a sensible resale value. The old maxim of prevention rather than cure was never truer than in connection with car servicing. Whether it be casting your eagle eye over the general workings of the car or getting down to the service task in a workmanlike (or workwomanlike) fashion, it's all going to be worthwhile in the long run. Remember that a worn part won't put itself right and isn't a thing to be lived with. Fix it as soon as you find it, even if it's not time for the next service.

In this Chapter, we've tried to present the servicing tasks in a logical way to minimize the amount of jacking up, etc, which may be a prelude to the actual job. The items listed are basically those recommended by the car manufacturers, but are supplemented by some additional ones which we think are well worth the extra trouble.

If you've recently bought the car, the safest thing is to go right through all the Service Schedules (not on the same day, of course!) unless you can really satisfy yourself that the previous owner was as meticulous about things as you'd like to be. You'll see that we've included Spring and Autumn check-ups, too, just so that you can make sure your car's as fit as possible for the season ahead.

Safety

Accidents do happen, but 99% of them can be prevented by taking a little care. We're going to list a few points which should reduce any accident risk, and we'd like you to read through them before starting work — it could prove to be very worthwhile.

DO wipe up grease or oil from the floor if you spill any (and you will do, sooner or later).

DO get someone to check regularly that everything's OK if you're likely to be spending some time underneath the car.

DON'T use a file or similar tool without a handle. The tang can give you a nasty gash if something goes wrong.

DO make sure when you're using a spanner, that it's the right size for the nut and that it's properly fitted before tightening or loosening.

DO brush away any drilling swarf with an old paintbrush — never your fingers.

DON'T allow battery acid or battery terminal corrosion to contact the skin or clothes. If it should happen, wash off immediately with plenty of cold running water.

DON'T rush any job — that's how mistakes are made. If you don't think you'll finish the job in time, do it tomorrow, but try not to make this an excuse for forgetting about it.

DO take care when pouring brake fluid. If it spills on the paintwork and isn't removed immediately, it'll take the paint off. And wash your hands well afterwards as it's poisonous.

DON'T run the engine in the garage with the doors closed.

DON'T work in an inspection pit with the engine running — the fumes will tend to concentrate at the lowest point.

DO keep long hair, sleeves, ties and the like well clear of any rotating parts when the engine's running.

DON'T grab hold of ignition HT leads when the engine's running — there's just the possibility of an electric shock, particularly if the leads are dirty or wet. **49**

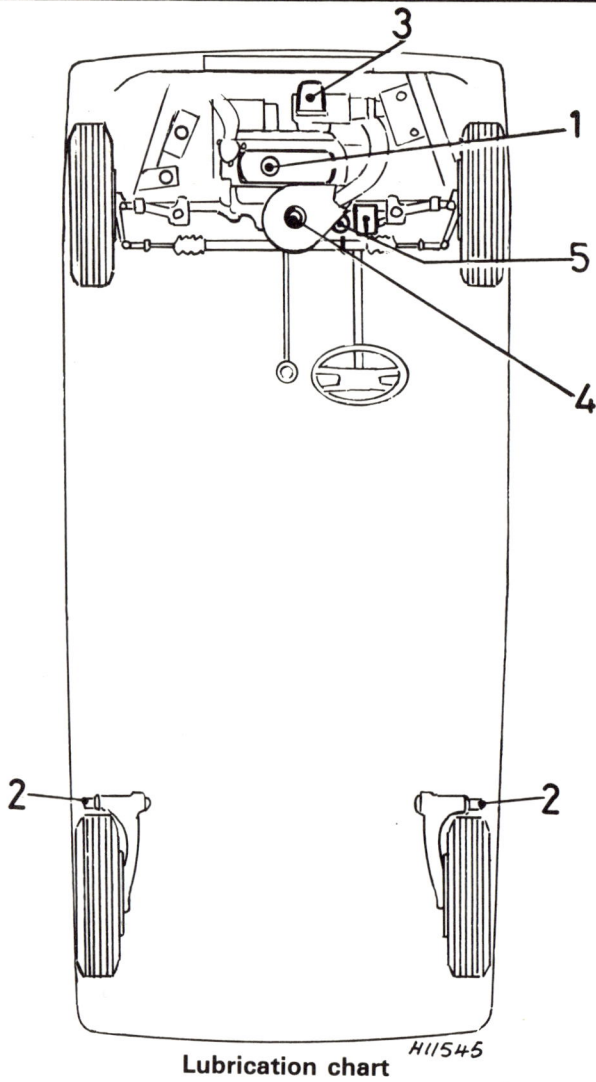

Lubrication chart

Component or system	Lubricant type or specification	Castrol product
Engine/transmission (1)	SAE 15W/50 multigrade engine oil	GTX
Suspension grease points (2)	Multi-purpose lithium based grease	LM Grease
Distributor (3)	SAE 15W/50 multigrade engine oil	GTX
Carburettor piston damper (4)	SAE 15W/50 multigrade engine oil	GTX
Brake and clutch fluid reservoir (5)	Hydraulic fluid to FMV SS 116 DOT 3 or SAE J1703c	Universal Brake and Clutch Fluid

DO chock the rear wheels when jacking up the front of the car and vice versa. Where possible, also apply the handbrake and engage first or reverse gear.

DON'T rely on the car jack when you're working underneath. Axle stands or wooden or concrete blocks should be used, but choose the points of support sensibly to prevent damaging anything.

SERVICE SCHEDULES
WEEKLY, BEFORE ANY LONG JOURNEY, OR EVERY 250 MILES

1 Check engine oil level (manual transmission models)

With the car parked on level ground, raise and support the bonnet. If the engine's been running, allow it to stand for a few minutes so that all oil can return to the sump before checking.

Withdraw the dipstick, which can be found in the front of the cylinder block in the middle. Wipe the end of the dipstick clean and fully reinsert it into its 'hole'. Withdraw it again and note the oil level mark in relation to the maximum and minimum marks on the dipstick. If necessary, top up using Castrol GTX or equivalent good quality multi-grade oil until the oil level aligns with the 'MAX' mark. Allow time for the oil to run down into the transmission casing before the final reading, and most important, avoid overfilling and wipe up any spilt oil.

1a Check engine oil (automatic transmission models)

The checking procedure's slightly different from that of the manual transmission models. If the car has been standing overnight, the level should be up to the 'HIGH' mark; if the engine has just been run, wait one minute after switching off, when the level should be up to the 'LOW' mark. Do not overfill.

2 Check coolant level

If the engine's been run up to or beyond its normal running temperature, great care must be taken when checking the coolant level in the expansion tank, since the coolant will be depressurised as soon as the cap is removed. Place a cloth over the cap and turn it *slowly* to the first stop position to allow the pressure to be released. Then depress the cap and turn it further to release and lift clear. Compress the radiator top hose with the hands and check the coolant movement within the expansion tank. If the level is below the half-full mark, add some coolant to fetch the level up to the correct line indicated, but remember if there's antifreeze in the system, any topping up should be done with an

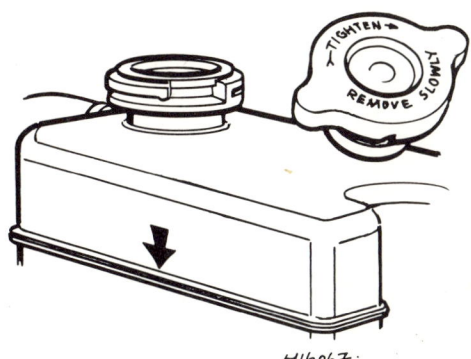

H16067

The coolant level mark in the expansion tank

equivalent mixture to keep the strength up. Continually adding water will dilute the mixture and weaken its effectiveness. Ensure that the cap's properly replaced. Check for leaks if you need to top up often.

3 Check tyre pressures

It's vitally important that the tyres are kept to the specified pressures, and they must therefore be checked each week. Under-inflation will badly affect the handling characteristics on the car and cause greater wear. In addition the tyre could, and probably will, overheat and irreparable damage could result. Over-inflation will cause a harsh ride and also greater wear.

The tyres should always be checked when they're cool and not after a high speed run when hot. Check the pressure of the spare at the same time and be sure that it's up to the highest pressure quoted for the front wheels.

4 Check battery electrolyte level

Whenever the battery is to be inspected or topped up, keep any naked flame away from it and **do not** smoke when checking, as the gases given off by the battery are explosive!

In most modern batteries the electrolyte level can be seen through the transparent casing. The level markings on the casing indicate whether the battery requires topping up. On batteries with patent troughs, glass balls and so on, follow the maker's instructions.

If the electrolyte level has dropped, remove the covers and add distilled or de-ionized water to each cell until the separators are just covered. At the same time, the top of the battery should be wiped clean with a dry cloth, to prevent the accumulation of dust and dampness which may cause the battery to become partially discharged over a period.

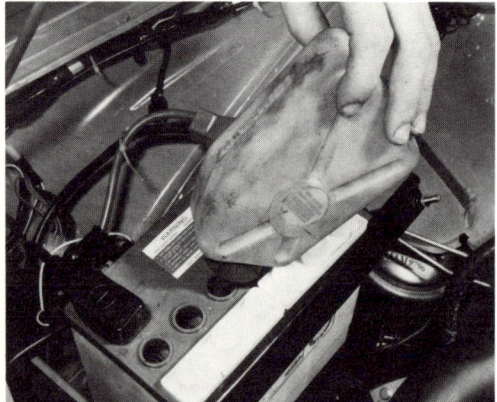

Top up the battery electrolyte level only if necessary

Check the condition and security of the battery terminals

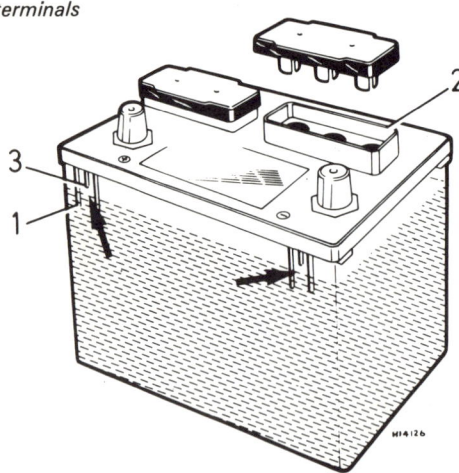

Electrolyte level marks (certain batteries only)

1   *Low mark*   3   *High mark*
2   *Filler trough*   *Arrows show electrolyte level*

In very cold weather the engine should be run to mix the distilled water with the electrolyte and prevent possible freezing. Any corrosion of the terminals can be cleaned using a dilute ammonia solution; then smear the terminals with a little petroleum jelly to prevent further corrosion.

5   Check windscreen/rear screen washer reservoirs

Check the level of the reservoir and, if necessary, top up with water, preferably using an additive which will help to remove greasy smears and squashed flies etc. In winter use an additive with antifreeze properties – **not** engine antifreeze.

Check the operation of the washers and if necessary adjust the washer jets by inserting a pin into the nozzle orifice and turning it accordingly.

Check the rear screen washer at the same time for satisfactory operation. The reservoir is located in the luggage compartment at the rear.

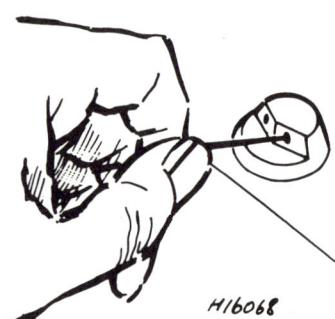

Windscreen washer jet cleaning and adjustment method

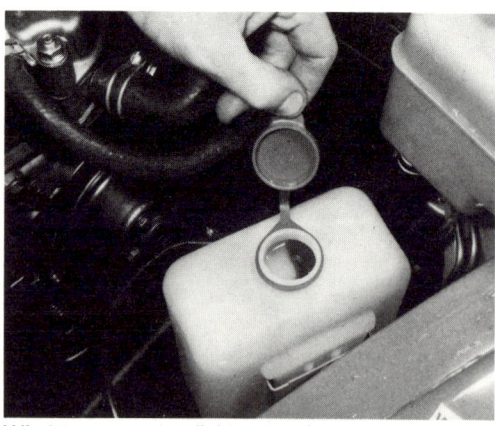

Windscreen washer fluid reservoir

6 Check brake/clutch fluid levels in reservoirs

Both the brake and (if applicable) the clutch fluid reservoirs must be checked regularly to ensure that the levels are correct. On the brake reservoir the fluid level is marked on the side of the translucent body, whilst on the clutch reservoir the fluid level must be kept up to the bottom of the filler neck.

Wipe the tops clean before removal and check that the ventilation hole's clear. Whenever you're topping up the brake or clutch fluid reservoirs, always use the specified fluid and ensure that no dirt's allowed to enter the reservoir. Don't spill any fluid over your hands or the car paintwork, and wash clean immediately if this should accidentally happen.

Regular topping up of either reservoir with any quantity of fluid indicates a leak in the system somewhere, and this must be investigated and the fault rectified at the earliest opportunity, for safety's sake.

7 Check tightness of wheel nuts

Using the flattened end of the wheelbrace, prise the hub covers from the wheels and check the respective wheel nuts for tightness. The recommended torque specified by the manufacturers is 42 lbf ft, but as you probably won't have a torque wrench, the nuts must be firmly tight but not over-tightened.

8 General checks

Operate the lights, indicators, windscreen wipers and washers to ensure that they all function correctly. If any light fails to function then the bulb has probably blown its filament and needs replacing. To do this refer to *In An Emergency.*

If more than one light's inoperative it may be that a fuse has blown or there's a bad connection. Should a fuse need renewal, be sure to replace it with a fuse of the specified value. Should this fuse blow again within a short period, the offending circuit must be inspected for the fault as soon as possible and the problem rectified.

EVERY 6000 MILES (10 000 KM OR 6 MONTHS – WHICHEVER COMES FIRST (AUTOMATIC TRANSMISSION MODELS ONLY)

1 Engine and transmission oil change and filter renewal

Prior to draining the oil, the engine should be run until its normal operating temperature has been reached; then park the car on level ground and switch off. Place a container of at least 10 pints underneath

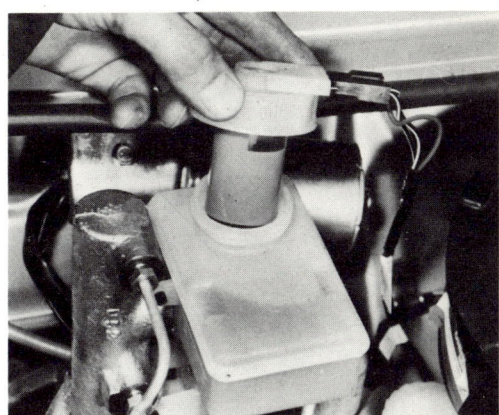

The brake fluid reservoir – remove cap as shown to top up level to 'MAX' mark if necessary

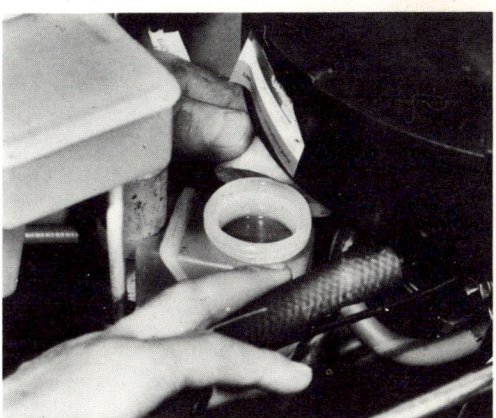

The clutch fluid reservoir shown with cap removed for topping up the fluid level

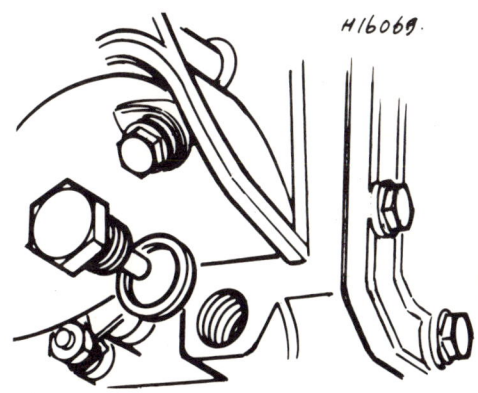

The engine/automatic transmission drain plug location

The oil filter cartridge location. On the MG variant the filter is suspended vertically downwards from the oil cooler

Removing the oil filter cartridge

the drain plug which is situated on the forward right-hand end of the transmission housing/sump.

Wipe the drain plug and surrounding area clean, and then carefully remove the plug (1 in AF spanner). The oil will gush forth almost horizontally at first, so keep your arm out of the way or you'll lubricate your elbow! Allow all the oil and sediment to drain out, and wipe the sump plug which has a magnetic inner face to attract and retain any metal particles which may be in the transmission/engine oil.

While the oil's draining, it's a good time to set about changing the oil filter. It's shown in the accompanying illustration. Unscrew the filter centre bolt to allow the filter container to be withdrawn. Allow for oil spillage by positioning a bowl or catch tray underneath. Extract and discard the old filter element and sealing ring, then clean out the container with paraffin and wipe dry: if necessary the through-bolt can be removed by extracting the circlip.

Renew the felt washer and ring seal if the old ones look damaged or worn. Always renew the main sealing ring in the filter head groove.

Assemble the new filter element and bowl and refit them, tightening the bolt moderately. Make sure the bowl sits in its groove and that the sealing ring is not kinked or pinched.

By now the oil should all have drained, so refit the sump plug, using a new washer if the existing one's damaged or deteriorated. Make sure the plug seals properly, but don't over-tighten or the transmission casing boss may fracture.

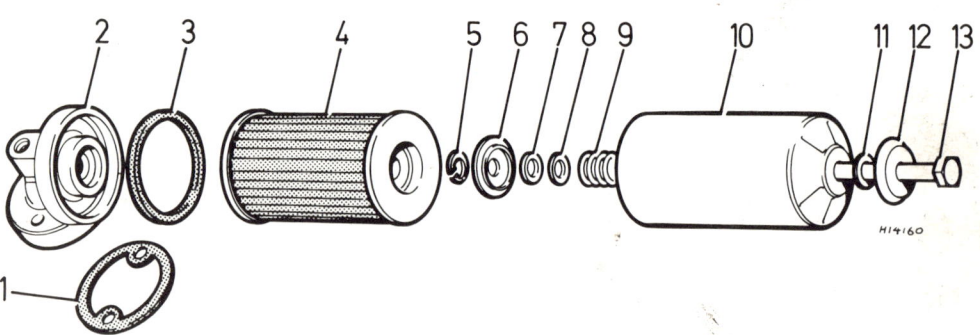

Oil filter components on automatic transmission models

1	Gasket	4	Element	7	Seal	10	Bowl
2	Head	5	Circlip	8	Washer	11	Felt washer
3	Sealing ring	6	Pressure plate	9	Spring	12	Collar
							13	Centre bolt

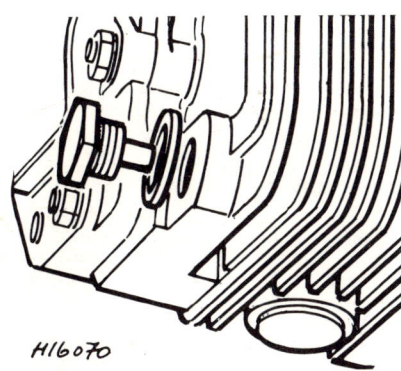

HI6070

The engine/manual transmission drain plug location

Refill the sump with the recommended grade and quantity of oil, taking care not to spill any over the exhaust manifold and not to overfill. Wipe any spillage up. Run the engine for a few minutes and then recheck the oil level. Make sure also that there are no leaks around the new filter joint.

2 Check the engagement of the transmission parking pawl

This is a task best entrusted to your BL dealer. Even though it may appear to function correctly, it is advisable to have this item checked, together with the selector cable and kickdown linkage adjustments, at regular intervals.

EVERY 12 000 MILES (20 000 KM) OR 12 MONTHS – WHICHEVER COMES FIRST

The list of service items below may seem a bit formidable compared with the simple weekly checks! There's nothing to stop you spreading the work over several weekends, of course, if that suits you better. At least it's only once a year.

If you're starting work on a cold engine, do the valve clearances (item 2) first, since they must be done with the engine cold. Then carry on until you have to go and buy something – it always happens! – and drain the oil when the engine's warmed up. If you're starting work on a hot engine, drain the oil first and leave the valve clearance check until things have cooled down a bit.

Under adverse operating conditions – mainly town work, or lots of towing – an extra oil change at 'half-time' (6000 miles/6 months) may be advisable. Consult your BL dealer if in doubt.

1 Renew engine/transmission oil and filter – all models

Commence draining the oil as described in the 6000-mile schedule. On manual transmission models, the oil filter is renewed as follows.

Place a container under the filter to catch any spilt oil. Wipe dry the oil filter cartridge and then unscrew it from the housing. You may need to use a strap wrench to unscrew it, although it should only be hand tight. Discard the filter on removal.

Wipe clean the sealing faces of the new oil filter cartridge and the filter head. Smear the sealing rubber with engine oil, then fit and tighten the cartridge *by hand only*. (If over-tightened, the seal may distort and you'll have real problems next time you try to remove the cartridge).

Refit the sump plug, using a new washer if the old one is damaged. Make sure that the plug seals properly, but don't overtighten it!

Refill the sump with the recommended grade and quantity of oil, wiping up any spillage. Run the engine for a few minutes, then recheck the oil level and inspect around the oil filter joint for any signs of leaks. Also inspect around the sump plug.

2 Check valve clearances and adjust if necessary

The valve clearances should be checked with the engine cold. Start by undoing the two special nuts which hold the valve cover on. Remove the nuts and washers and put them somewhere safe. Rock the valve cover back and forth to break the seal, then lift the cover away. (You may need to disconnect the vacuum hose which runs to the distributor – in which case, make a note to reconnect it!) If you're lucky, the cork gasket will stay in one piece, either in the cover or on the head. It's as well to have a spare one handy.

With the cover removed, study the valvegear now exposed. The valve at the pulley end of the engine is No 1, and the valve at the other end is No 8. You will see that two of the valve springs are being compressed by their rocker arms. These valves are open.

Turn the engine until No 8 valve is open. (You can turn the engine with a big spanner on the crankshaft pulley bolt, or by engaging top gear and pushing the car backwards or forwards. Either way, it'll be easier if you take the spark plugs out – see item 8). Try to insert a feeler gauge of the specified thickness – see *Vital Statistics* – between the rocker arm and the valve stem on No 1 valve. The feeler blade should be a firm sliding fit. If it's at all slack, or (worse) too tight, adjust as follows.

Slacken the locknut at the other end of the rocker arm concerned. A ring spanner is good for this. Watch your knuckles! Now keep the ring spanner on the **55**

Removing the valve (rocker) cover (MG type shown)

Checking and adjusting the valve clearances

locknut, the feeler gauge between the rocker arm and valve stem, and turn the adjusting screw inwards (clockwise) to decrease the clearance, outwards (anti-clockwise) to increase it. A third hand, most likely belonging to an assistant, is useful. Keep sliding the feeler blade back and forth until you judge that a firm sliding fit has been achieved. Hold the adjusting screw still with the screwdriver and tighten the locknut firmly. Recheck the clearance — if the adjusting screw moved, slacken the locknut again and correct matters. Valve clearances are important — too tight and you'll burn valves out, too slack and the engine will be noisy and inefficient — so take the time to get them right.

Repeat the procedure on the other seven valves, using the table below. You'll need to turn the engine 180° (half a turn) after each pair of valves has been done. You will also notice that the numbers of the

valve open and the valve to be adjusted always add up to 9 — this is the 'rule of nine' method which you may hear mentioned.

Valve open	Adjust valve
8	1 (exhaust)
6	3 (inlet)
4	5 (exhaust)
7	2 (inlet)
1	8 (exhaust)
3	6 (inlet)
5	4 (exhaust)
2	7 (inlet)

Go round the sequence once more, rechecking the clearances, then refit the valve cover. Use a new gasket if necessary — you can lose a surprising amount of oil through a cracked or over-compressed gasket — and wipe any sludge from inside the cover first. (The oil filler cap goes towards the timing chain (pulley) end of the engine, unless it's centrally placed as on the MG). Fit the washers and special nuts and tighten the nuts — don't overdo it or you'll squash the cover, just do them up enough to nip the gasket firmly.

3 Renew air cleaner element

This may be necessary more frequently if you live in a very dirty region, or have just driven across the Sahara. Start by removing the two wing nuts from the top of the air cleaner — that's the big round box on top of the carburettor. Prise the lid off the box if you've got one like we show in the photos — otherwise, pull the whole cleaner away, separating it from the hot air shroud tube, and remove the cover by releasing the lugs.

Lift out the old element and discard it. Wipe clean the inside and lid of the cleaner box, then insert the new element and refit the lid. If the complete air cleaner has been removed, you may as well delay refitting it until you've completed some more of the items below.

4 Top up carburettor dashpot

Unscrew the cap from the top of the carburettor suction chamber and carefully pull out the piston damper, which is attached to the cap. Squirt clean engine oil into the hole in the top of the suction chamber until the level is about half an inch (13 mm) above the top of the hollow piston rod, then reinsert the damper and screw up the cap.

While you're at it, put a spot of engine oil on the moving parts of the throttle and choke linkages at the carburettor end — get somebody to work the controls for you if you're not sure which bits move. Also check that the fuel lines are secure and in good condition.

Prise free and remove the air cleaner lid ...

... for access to the element

Topping up the carburettor piston damper with engine oil

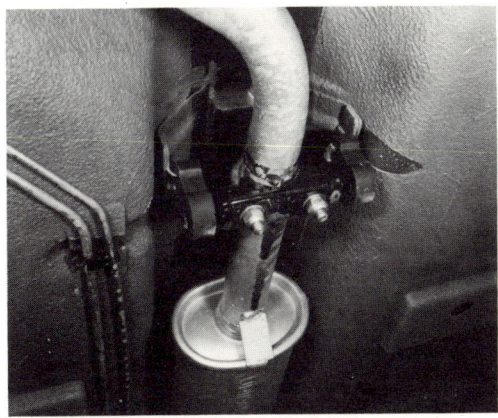

Exhaust system intermediate mounting – check condition and security

5 Exhaust system inspection

This inspection is best carried out with the vehicle on ramps or positioned over a pit, but if these are not available, raise and support the vehicle at one end to provide sufficient clearance underneath. To save having to raise the vehicle again later, you may wish to leave this operation until you are ready to check other items such as the brakes, steering and suspension.

Check the exhaust pipe and silencer for security and signs of deterioration. Any small leaks may be temporarily repairable using Holts 'Gun-Gum' or similar silencer sealer. Larger holes are best patched using a special silencer bandage, but remember that this can only be a temporary repair and a new silencer and/or pipe will be needed pretty soon.

6 Check condition of cooling system and heater hoses

Normally, providing that the water level's correctly maintained and the system's occasionally drained to remove any accumulation of sediment, the cooling system should seldom give trouble. Leaks can sometimes prove difficult to check but not impossible. Inspect the radiator top hose, bottom hose, expansion tank hose and the two heater hoses for signs of cracking, leaking or softening and fit new hoses as necessary. If a leak occurs around a hose, tightening the hose clip may be all that's necessary but sometimes this will make the leak worse. The remedy is to fit a clip of the worm drive type and to tighten it just sufficiently to prevent leakage.

Fitting new radiator hoses is a straightforward operation but the cooling system will have to be drained. Details of this will be found in the 24 000-mile Schedule. If a new hose is difficult to place on its union, lubricate with a little soap.

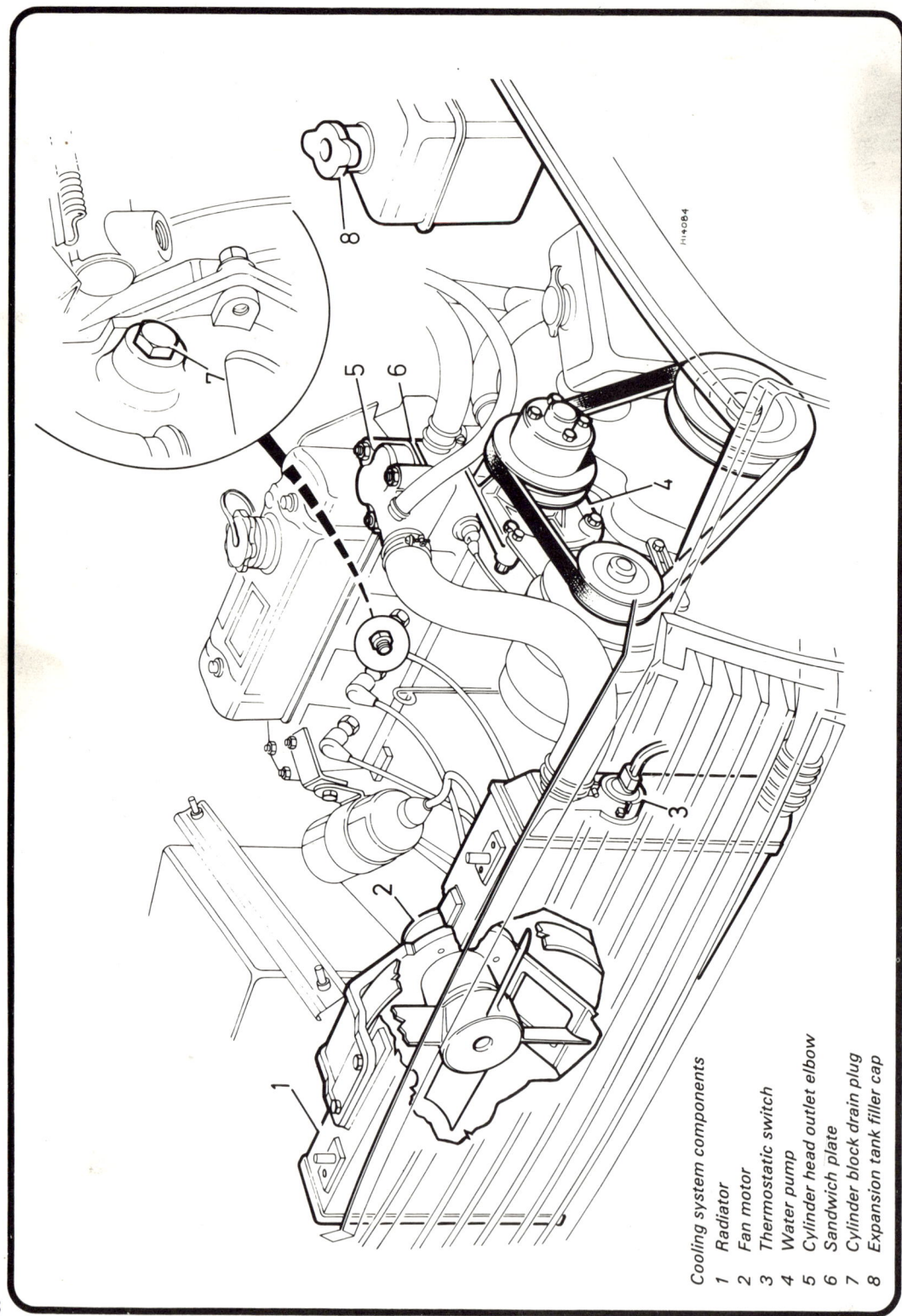

Cooling system components

1 Radiator
2 Fan motor
3 Thermostatic switch
4 Water pump
5 Cylinder head outlet elbow
6 Sandwich plate
7 Cylinder block drain plug
8 Expansion tank filler cap

If the radiator's leaking slightly it may be cured by using Holts Radweld. This is poured into the radiator when the coolant's hot and the engine's then allowed to tick over for a few minutes to circulate the mixture. The leak will gradually diminish as the additive comes into contact with the air and will finally cease, giving a relatively permanent seal. This additive is also useful for sealing small leaks from cracks in the cylinder head or block.

7 Check and adjust the distributor contact breaker points

To clean and adjust the contact breaker points, first release the two spring clips securing the distributor cap and lift it off, tucking it to one side complete with HT leads. Lift off the rotor arm from the cam spindle.

Wipe clean the inside of the distributor cap using a dry, clean cloth, and inspect the cap carefully for signs of any fine hairline cracks. The electrical contacts must be in reasonable condition and any carbon deposit on them may be scraped off using a small penknife. Renew the cap if it's at all suspect.

Prise open the contact breaker points and inspect the faces for signs of uneven or excessive wear. If the contact faces are pitted or dirty they can be removed and cleaned or, if necessary, renewed, although normally this is only required at 24 000-mile intervals. If the contact breaker points need to be removed for renovation or renewal, refer to the 24 000-mile service schedule for details.

If the contact points do not show excessive pitting or wear, rotate the cam spindle so that the high point of a cam lobe is beneath the heel of the moving contact point (so that the points are fully opened). To rotate the cam spindle to the exact point required, use the same method as when checking the valve clearances (item 2). Turn the engine until the points are fully open – that is, so that movement forwards or backwards will cause the gap to close up.

When the contact points are fully opened, insert a clean feeler gauge of the specified thickness (see *Vital Statistics*) and check that the gap is as given. The selected blade should be a sliding fit between the contacts.

Should the clearance be incorrect, loosen the points securing screw, then insert a screwdriver into the notch at the end of the contact set baseplate and lever against the pip to make the adjustment in the desired direction. Retighten the securing screw and recheck the clearance. Finer adjustment of the contact points setting may be made using a dwell meter, if available, in accordance with its maker's instructions. This is particularly desirable for the Ducellier distributor.

Check the distributor cap condition and the lead connections

Check the contact breaker points clearance using a feeler gauge

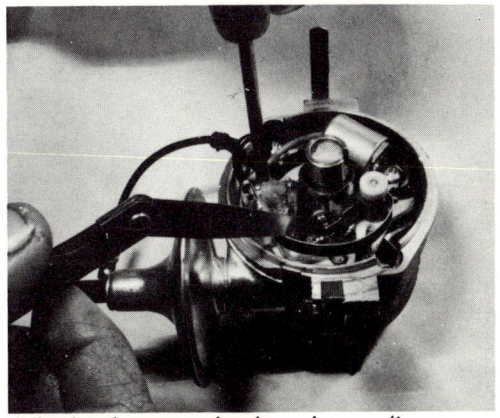

Adjusting the contact breaker points gap (Lucas distributor shown)

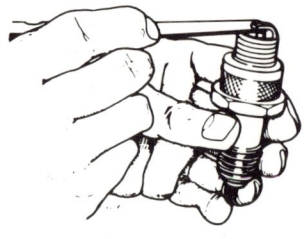

Checking plug gap with feeler
gauges

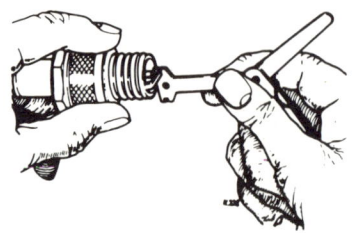

Altering the plug gap. Note use
of correct tool

Spark plug maintenance

White deposits and damaged
porcelain insulation indicating
overheating

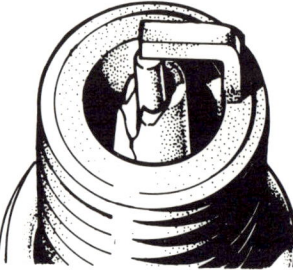

Broken porcelain insulation
due to bent central electrode

Electrodes burnt away due to
wrong heat value or chronic
pre-ignition (pinking)

Excessive black deposits
caused by over-rich mixture
or wrong heat value

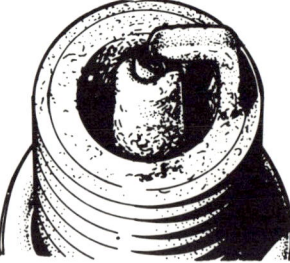

Mild white deposits and electrode burnt indicating too
weak a fuel mixture

Plug in sound condition with
light greyish brown deposits

Spark plug electrode conditions

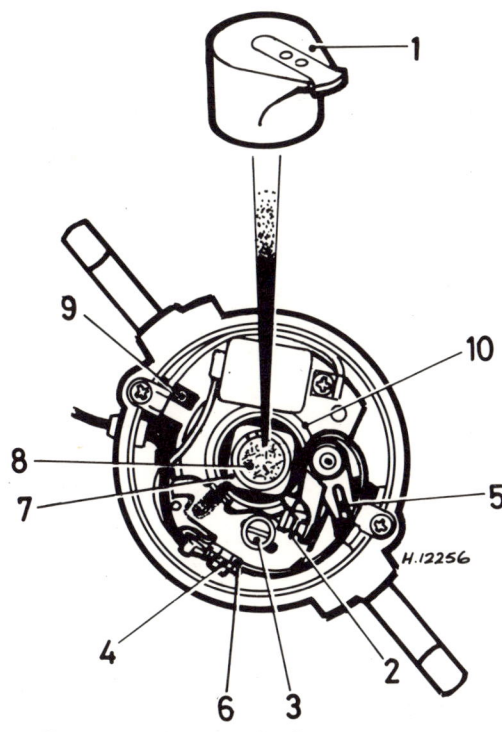

Top view of the Lucas distributor with the cap removed

1   Rotor arm
2   Contact points
3   Retaining screw
4   Terminal plate (black wire at top)
5   Baseplate peg
6   Insulator shoe
7   Cam (lightly smear with grease)
8   Felt pad (apply a few drops of oil)
9   Lubrication hole for centrifugal weights mechanism (a few drops)
10 Moving plate groove (1 drop of oil every 24 000 miles)

On the Lucas distributor, lightly wipe the cam with grease and apply a few drops of oil into the felt pad within the cam spindle. A few drops of oil should also be applied through the baseplate to lubricate the centrifugal weights mechanism. Wipe up any surplus lubricant.

On the Ducellier distributor, the cam is also lightly smeared with grease and the pressure pad of the moving contact must also be lubricated with grease. Lubricate the felt pad in the top of the cam spindle with a few drops of oil, then rotate the crankshaft so that one of the centrifugal weight pivot posts can be seen when looking through the

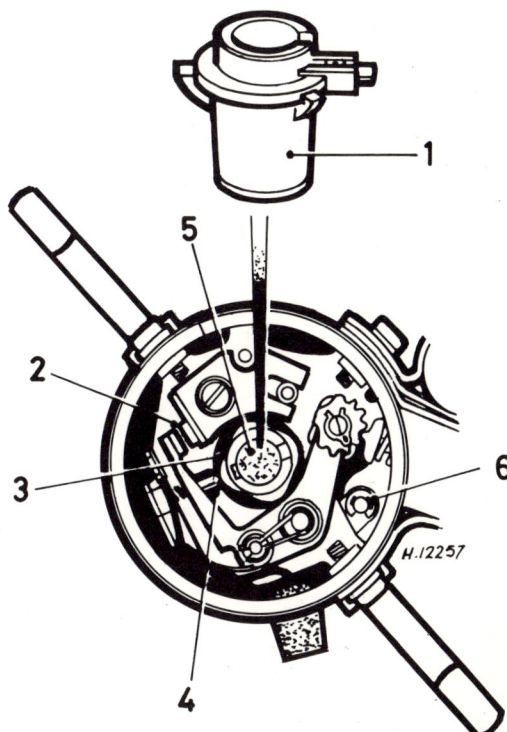

Top view of the Ducellier distributor with cap removed

1   Rotor arm
2   Contact breaker points
3   Cam (lightly smear with grease)
4   Pressure pad (lubricate with grease)
5   Felt pad (apply a few drops of oil)
6   Pivot post exposed in cut-out

baseplate cut-out. Apply one drop of oil at this point, then turn the engine so that the opposite post can also be lubricated. Wipe up any surplus lubricant.

Refit the rotor arm and distributor cap. Wipe clean all the HT leads, not forgetting the coil tower, and check both HT and LT leads for security and freedom from cracks. Don't put the old spark plugs back though, as the next task is ...

8   Renew the spark plugs

Check that the plug caps or leads are numbered 1 to 4 (with No 1 at the pulley end of the engine) — if not, label the caps yourself with tape or paint spots. Pull the caps off the plugs. Wipe clean the area round the base of each plug.

Unscrew and remove each plug in turn, using a proper spark plug spanner. Although you're going to renew the plugs, it's worth studying the condition of **61** the old ones to see if there are any warning signs of engine wear or maladjustment. The accompanying illustration gives some idea of what to look for.

Take the new plugs out of their packets and use a feeler gauge to check that the electrode gap is as given in *Vital Statistics*. If necessary, alter the gap by bending the side electrode – **not** the centre electrode, as this will crack the insulation.

Put a smear of grease or anti-seize compound on the plug threads and screw them into their holes. You should be able to screw them in by hand until they're home, then tighten a further quarter of a turn – or more – with the spark plug spanner. Push the plug caps back onto the plugs, making sure that the leads and caps are clean and dry, and that the leads are connected to the correct plugs!

9   Check ignition timing

As the contact breaker heel wears, or after a new contact has been fitted, there may be a slight shift of ignition timing – the moment at which the spark occurs. Checking the timing statically (that's with the engine stopped) is easily done. If you want a more accurate setting, you must use a stroboscopic light (this is dynamic timing); the light will be supplied with operating instructions and you'll find it quite easy to use but, if you haven't got one, dynamic timing's a job for the local garage.

Test bulb method

Remove the No 1 spark plug (crankshaft pulley end) and place the thumb over the aperture, then turn the engine in the normal running direction (clockwise from crankshaft pulley end) until pressure is felt in No 1 cylinder, indicating that the piston is commencing its compression stroke. Use a spanner on the crankshaft pulley bolt, or engage top gear and pull the car forwards on manual gearbox models.

Continue turning the engine until the V-notch in the crankshaft pulley is exactly in line with the timing cover pointer representing 4° BTDC. Note that the large pointer indicates top dead centre (TDC) and the remaining pointer peaks are in increments of 4° BTDC.

Remove the distributor cap and check that the rotor arm is pointing in the direction of the No 1 terminal of the cap. Connect a 12 volt test bulb between the end of the moving contact spring and a suitable earthing point on the engine.

Loosen the distributor clamp plate bolt (at the base of the distributor).

Switch on the ignition. If the bulb is already lit, turn the distributor body slightly anti-clockwise until the bulb goes out. Turn the distributor body clockwise until the bulb *just* lights up, indicating that the points have just opened. Tighten the clamp bolt.

Switch off the ignition and remove the test bulb.

The ignition timing mark pointers on the timing chest and the crankshaft pulley timing notch, in this instance aligned with the 0° pointer (TDC)

Refit the distributor cap and No 1 spark plug and HT lead. Once the engine has been started, check the timing stroboscopically as follows and adjust as necessary.

Stroboscopic timing light method

Disconnect and plug the vacuum pipe at the distributor. Wipe clean the crankshaft pulley notch and timing cover pointers. If necessary use white paint or chalk to highlight the marks.

Connect the timing light to the engine in accordance with the manufacturer's instructions (usually between No 1 spark plug and HT lead).

If not so equipped, connect a tachometer to the engine in accordance with the manufacturer's instructions, then start the engine and run it at 1500 rpm.

Point the timing light at the timing marks and they should appear to be stationary with the crank pulley notch in alignment with the appropriate mark; refer to *Vital Statistics* for the ignition timing applicable to the engine being worked on. Note that the large pointer indicates top dead centre (TDC) and the remaining pointer peaks are in increments of 4° BTDC. **Take care** not to get anything caught in the moving parts of the engine, and keep clear of the cooling fan in case it starts up unexpectedly.

If adjustment is necessary (ie the pulley notch does not line up with the appropriate mark), loosen the distributor clamp plate bolt and turn the body clockwise to advance and anti-clockwise to retard the ignition timing. Tighten the bolt when the setting is correct.

Gradually increase the engine speed while still pointing the timing light at the timing marks. The pulley notch should appear to move anti-clockwise proving that the centrifugal weights are operating correctly. If the ignition advance is not in accordance

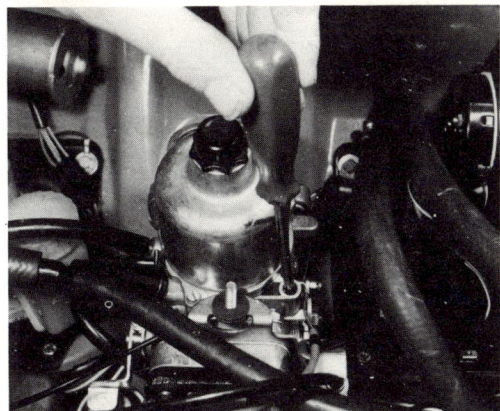

Adjusting the engine idle speed

Adjusting the mixture control

with the information given in the Specifications, the distributor should be overhauled and a check made of the centrifugal mechanism.

Switch off the engine and remove the timing light and tachometer. Reconnect the vacuum pipe to the distributor. Disconnect the pipe from the carburettor and remove the distributor cap. Suck on the end of the pipe and check that the baseplate (Lucas) or pivot link (Ducellier) moves to advance the points. If not, the vacuum unit may be faulty.

Refit the distributor cap and vacuum pipe.

10 Check carburettor adjustment

Before you lay a screwdriver on the carburettor, a few words of caution. It shouldn't be necessary to make much adjustment to any of the carburettor settings if the rest of the engine and the ignition system are properly maintained. There's certainly no point in trying to adjust the carb until the valve clearances have been checked, along with the ignition timing, points gap and spark plugs. When you have

good grounds for believing the mixture adjustment to be incorrect, stick to checking and adjusting the idle speed; and don't move any 'tamperproof' devices if the car's still under warranty, or where their removal is forbidden by law.

Connect a tachometer to the engine in accordance with the manufacturer's instructions. If not already done, remove the air cleaner (item 3) and top up the carburettor dashpot (item 4). Check that there is a little slack in the choke cable – 0.08 in (2 mm) is the theoretical value. Warm the engine up if running it until the cooling fan cuts in, then proceed as follows.

Increase the engine speed to 2500 rpm for 30 seconds. This will clear any excess fuel from the manifold. Repeat this at three-minute intervals during the adjustment procedure.

Allow the engine to idle and check the idle speed (see *Vital Statistics)* If necessary, turn the throttle adjusting screw (on top of the carburettor) clockwise to increase the speed, anti-clockwise to reduce it.

Pull the choke control knob out until the arrow on the fast idle cam is aligned with the fast idle adjusting screw, then check the fast idle speed. Turn the adjusting screw if necessary to achieve the correct speed.

If mixture adjustment is necessary, prise out the tamperproof plug (where fitted) which covers the mixture adjusting screw. To adjust the idling mixture, slowly turn the mixture screw, located on the right-hand side of the carburettor, clockwise (to enrich) or anti-clockwise (to weaken), until a point is reached where the engine speed is fastest. Slowly turn the mixture screw anti-clockwise until the engine speed just commences to drop.

Turn the throttle adjustment screw to regain the specified idling speed. Remove the tachometer and **refit the air cleaner.**

Check condition and tension adjustment of the drivebelt

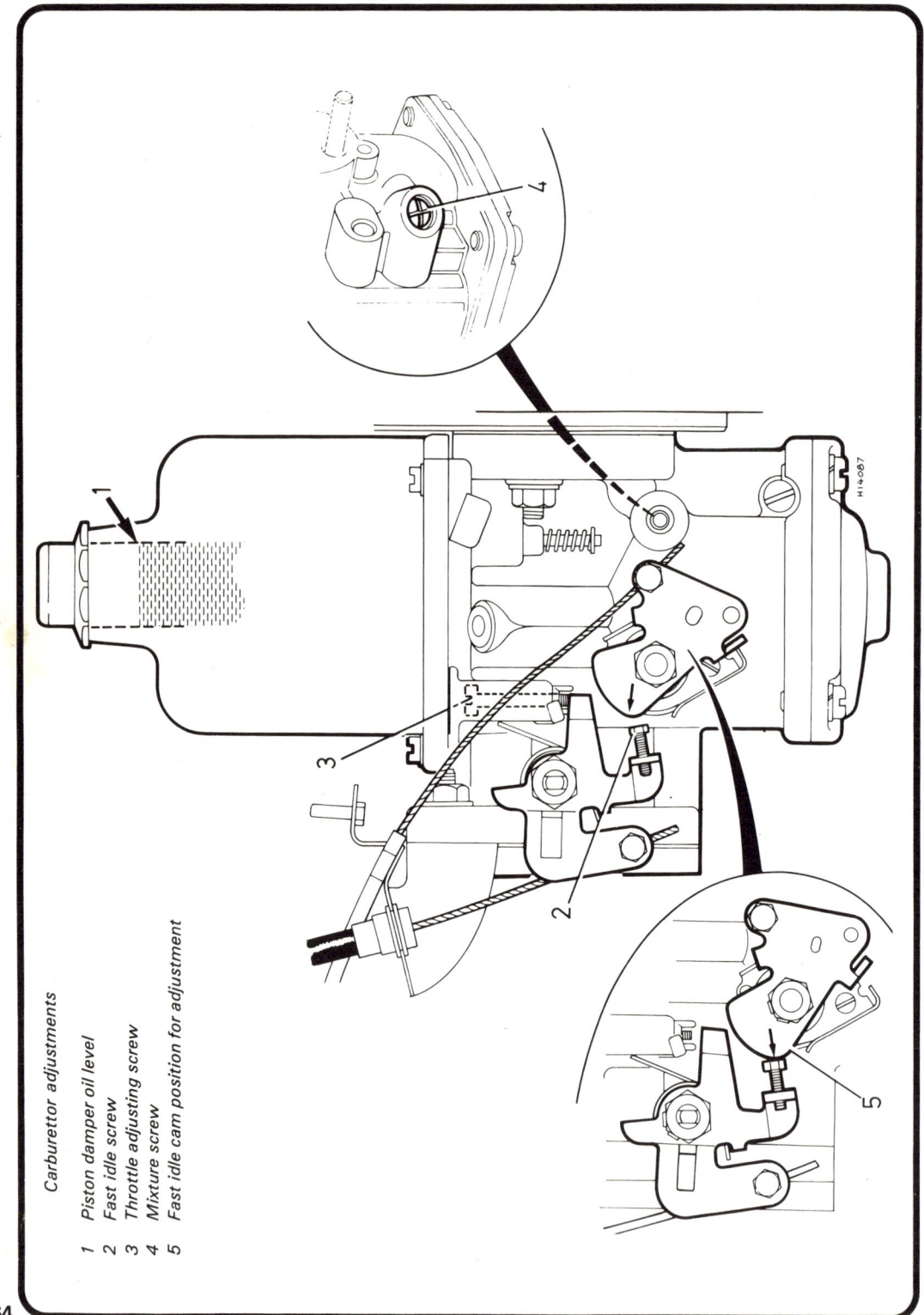

Carburettor adjustments

1   Piston damper oil level
2   Fast idle screw
3   Throttle adjusting screw
4   Mixture screw
5   Fast idle cam position for adjustment

64

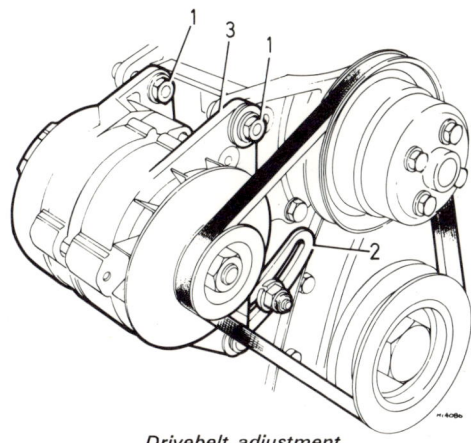

Drivebelt adjustment

1   Alternator pivot   3   Alternator drive
    bolts   end bracket
2   Adjusting link

11 Check tension and condition of alternator/water pump drivebelt

The belt is connected round the crankshaft pulley and drives the alternator and coolant pump.

Examine the belt for signs of fraying. If there are any, then the belt will have to be renewed. To do this slacken the alternator adjusting and mounting bolts and push the alternator in towards the engine. The belt can then be slipped off the pulley flanges and removed. Fit the new belt, using the fingers to manipulate it. Never attempt to remove or fit a drivebelt by levering it over a pulley rim without having first released the alternator adjuster and mounting bolts.

Adjustment of drivebelt tension is carried out in the following way. Release the alternator bolts (or tighten slightly if a new belt has just been fitted) until the alternator can be pivoted stiffly, and then pull outwards away from the engine until, using moderate thumb pressure at the centre point of the longest run of the belt, total deflection of 0.16 in (4 mm) is obtained. Tighten the alternator bolts without disturbing the adjustment. If a new belt has been fitted, check the adjustment again after 500 miles (800 km) running.

12 Check clutch return stop clearance (early models only)

On earlier manual transmission models, the clutch return stop clearance should be checked and adjusted if necessary. (Later models do not have this stop and are self-adjusting).

Pull the release lever out against the tension of the slave cylinder return spring until all the free

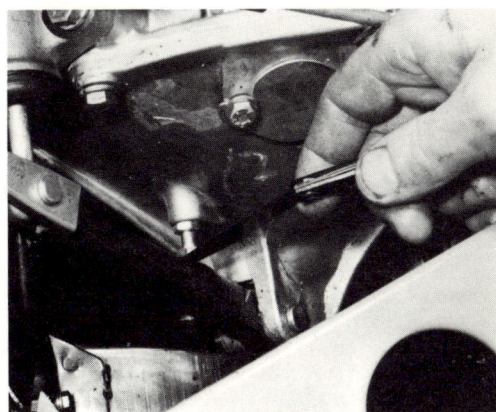

Checking the clutch return stop clearance (early models)

movement is taken up. Using a feeler blade, check that the clearance between the return stop and release lever is 0.04 in (1 mm). If not, loosen the locknut and reposition the return stop screw as necessary, then tighten the locknut. Make sure that the lever is held against the spring tension during the adjustment.

Before finishing with the clutch, inspect the hydraulic pipes and hoses for security and any signs of fluid leakage.

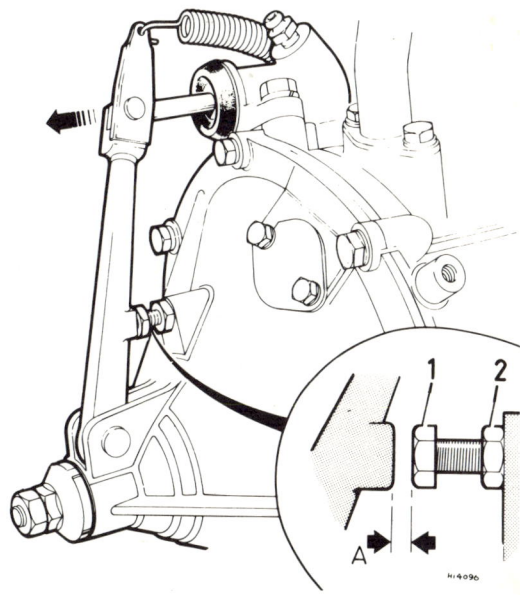

Clutch adjustment – earlier models only

1   Return stop   A   Return stop
2   Locknut   clearance

13 Check the battery leads and terminals

Disconnect and clean the battery terminals and leads. After refitting them and before fitting the plastic covers, smear the exposed metal with petroleum jelly.

At the same time, inspect the battery bar and carrier for corrosion. If evident, remove the battery and clean the deposits away, then treat the affected metal with a proprietary cleaner anti-rust liquid and paint with the original colour.

When the battery is removed for whatever reason, it is worthwhile checking it for cracks and leakage. Cracks can be caused by topping up the cells with distilled water in winter *after* instead of *before* a run. This gives the water no chance to mix with the electrolyte, so the former freezes and splits the battery case. If the battery case is fractured, it may be possible to repair it with a proprietary compound, but this depends on the material used for the case.

14 Brakes, steering and suspension checks — general

The following operations require the vehicle to be raised for inspection. To avoid having to continuously raise and lower the vehicle at each end or corner as applicable, it is best if you raise and support the vehicle at one end and complete all the checks at that end. Then lower the vehicle and complete the checks at the other end. Be sure to support the vehicle with safety stands while working underneath it. Start with the front end components, jack up the front end, apply the handbrake and locate the axle stands under the correct points — see *In an Emergency*.

15 Check front brake pads and discs for wear

Remove the front roadwheel on each side for access to the disc calipers. Using a screwdriver, move the anti-rattle spring upwards to release it from the bottom split pin, then withdraw it downwards from the upper split pin.

Measure the thickness of the lining material on each disc pad, and if either one is at or below the specified minimum (see *Vital Statistics*) renew the complete set of front disc pads. Note that the instrument panel warning lamp should glow if either inner pad wears to the minimum thickness.

To remove the pads, straighten the split pins and extract them from the caliper. Disconnect the wear indicator wiring from the harness and detach the rubber clip. Press each pad slightly against its pistons, then withdraw it from the caliper using pliers.

Brush the dust and dirt from the caliper, pistons, disc and pads, *but do not inhale it as it is injurious to health*. Scrape any scale or rust from the disc and pad backing plate.

Removing the disc pad anti-rattle spring

The disc brake pad wear indicator wiring connector

Removing the disc pad from the caliper

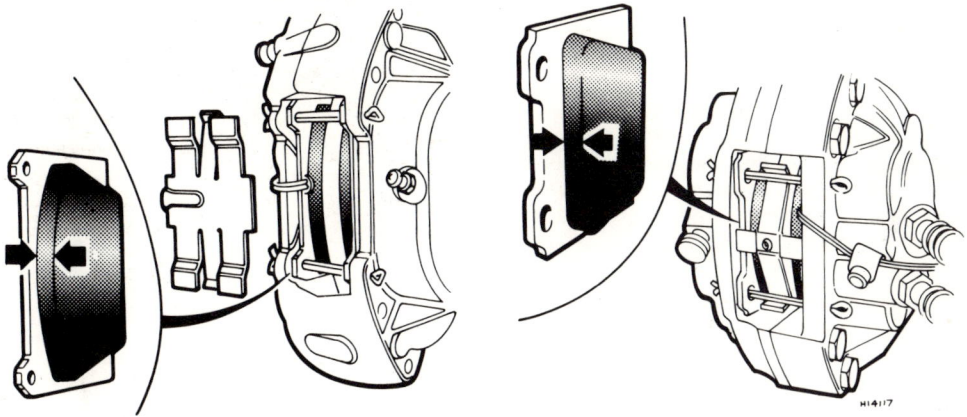

Alternative types of front brake pads – arrows indicate pad thickness measuring point

Using a piece of wood, press the pistons back into the caliper. At the same time check the level of brake fluid in the reservoir; if this is near the top of the reservoir, unscrew the relevant bleed screw to release the fluid while the piston is being depressed. Tighten it immediately afterwards.

Smear brake grease lightly on the metal-to-metal contact surfaces of each pad backing plate. Insert the pads into the caliper with the linings facing the disc. Note that only one pad has a wear indicator; fit this on the inner side of the disc.

Reconnect the pad wear indicator wiring and clip. Insert the split pins through the caliper and pads and bend the ends to secure. Refit the anti-rattle spring under the lower split pin, then hook it under the top split pin.

This procedure is then repeated on the opposite front wheel caliper. On completion depress the foot-brake pedal several times to set the pads, then check and, if necessary, top up the level of brake fluid in the master cylinder resrvoir.

Do not refit the roadwheels just yet, as other checks at the front end can be made with them removed for better access.

16 Check that the brake pad wear warning indicators are operational

To do this check, locate the twin terminal black plastic sockets situated on the wiring harness over each wheel arch. Switch on the ignition and connect a bridging wire between the terminals of one socket; the pad wear warning light should be illuminated on the instrument panel. If not, either the warning bulb is blown or there is a fault in the circuit. Repeat the check on the remaining front brake.

17 Check braking system pipes and hoses

Make a visual inspection of the brake servo hose for condition and security (1.3 models only).

Visually inspect the respective hydraulic lines from the master cylinder to the front and rear brake units, looking for any signs of corrosion, leaks or damage. If any item is found to be defective, have your BL dealer check and if necessary renew the part concerned without delay.

18 Lubricate and inspect steering and front suspension components

Whilst the vehicle is still raised and supported, lubricate the front suspension pivot each side using a grease gun. Apply several strokes of the gun to each nipple in turn. Now examine the following items on each side:

(a) *Check the Hydragas units and lines for leaks*

(b) *Check the rack-and-pinion unit for security and damage*

(c) *Check the steering joints and arms for wear and damage*

(d) *Check the steering gaiters for splits and leakage*

(e) *Check the driveshaft gaiters for splits and leakage*

(f) *Check the front suspension joints and mountings for wear and damage*

The front wheel alignment must also be checked at this mileage, but this is a task to be entrusted to your BL dealer or (maybe) a tyre specialist.

On completion of these checks the front road-wheels can be refitted and the wheel bearings checked for wear by trying to rock the wheel as **67**

Front suspension pivot grease nipple location (arrowed)

shown in the photo. Investigate any movement.

You may wish to interchange the positions of the wheels to even out the tyre wear, but remember that with radial tyres it's recommended that the tyres are only moved from front to rear and vice versa on the *same side* of the vehicle, and not from side to side. The spare can be brought into the sequence if required, but mark the 'new' spare wheel so you'll know to which side to fit it when its turn comes again for running on the road.

It's a worthwhile idea to have your wheels rebalanced about halfway through their useful life, to offset loss of tread since they were originally balanced. Whether you have them balanced on or off the vehicle is a matter of choice – on-car balancing is more efficient, but off the car is less restrictive in that you don't have to worry about marking the wheels before removing them during repairs and maintenance.

Steering vibration or steering wheel judder at certain road speeds is nearly always due to the front wheels being out of balance. In severe cases a tyre tread can be worn away in a very short distance.

19 Check rear brake linings for wear

How quickly the rear brake linings wear will depend on how and where you live – and how often you drive away with the handbrake on! – but once a year is not too often to look at them, to check both for wear and for other potentially dangerous faults.

Chock the front wheels, slacken the rear wheel nuts and jack up the rear of the car. Support the car with axle stands and remove the rear wheels. Release the handbrake.

Remove the two cross-head screws which secure the brake drum. Find the brake adjuster – it's the square-headed thing sticking out of the rear of the

backplate, at the top. Give the adjuster a shot of releasing fluid or penetrating oil, then unscrew it (anti-clockwise viewed from the centre of the car), preferably using the proper brake adjuster spanner. Don't remove the adjuster, just unscrew it a few turns.

You should now be able to pull the brake drum off over the wheel studs. If it's reluctant to move, and the adjuster is fully released (and the handbrake off!) it may be necessary to tap behind the rim of the drum with a wooden or plastic hammer. Work round the rim of the drum, tapping gently. *Don't* use a metal hammer, unless you put a block of wood between the hammer head and the drum, as the drum is quite brittle.

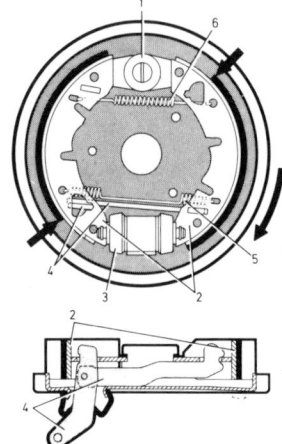

Sectional view of the rear brakes

1 Adjuster	5 Bottom return
2 Brake shoes	spring
3 Wheel cylinder	6 Top return
4 Handbrake lever	spring
assembly	

Arrows indicate brake shoe leading edges and forward rotation of drum

With the brake drum removed, wipe or brush out the dust from the brake drum, brake shoes, and backplate, *but do not inhale it as it is injurious to health*. Scrape any scale or rust from the drum.

Measure the brake shoe lining thickness. If it is worn down to the specified minimum amount, or if it is nearly worn down to the rivets, you will need to renew *all four* brake shoes at the rear. You will also need to renew them (and to fix the leak!) if they are contaminated with grease from a leaking rear hub bearing seal or hydraulic fluid from a leaking wheel cylinder. Renewal of the rear hub seals and wheel cylinder seals is dealt with in the Haynes Owners Workshop Manual for the Metro.

Check for play in the front wheel bearings when the wheels are in position as shown

Remove the retaining screws to withdraw the brake drum

General view of the rear brake assembly with the drum removed

If the linings are in good condition, refit the drums and then adjust the brakes as described in the next item. If, however, the linings are in need of renewal, they are removed together with the brake shoes as follows.

First note the location of the return springs, and to which holes they are fitted (refer to the accompanying illustration). Release each shoe from the adjuster pegs using a screwdriver or adjustable spanner. Similarly release the shoes from the wheel cylinder pistons. Disengage the handbrake levers and withdraw the shoes. Detach both return springs.

Do not touch the brake pedal or handbrake lever while the shoes are removed. Position an elastic band over the wheel cylinder pistons to retain them.

Lay the new shoes on a flat surface in their approximate fitted attitude. The leading edges must face in the opposite direction to forward movement of the drum (see the illustration).

Hook the bottom return spring to the shoes with the middle section to the bottom; this will ensure that it does not foul the hub when fitted. Fit the shoes and spring to the handbrake levers. Remove the elastic band and locate the shoe webs in the wheel cylinder piston slots.

Hook the top return spring to the shoes from the rear, then lever the shoe webs into the adjuster peg slots.

Fully unscrew the adjuster. Tap the shoes so that they are located concentric to the hub.

Fit the drum and tighten the two screws, then adjust the rear brakes as given below.

20 Check the rear brake and handbrake adjustments

With the car raised and supported at the rear, ensure that the handbrake is fully released and check that both rear wheels can be rotated freely.

Working beneath the car turn the adjuster on the rear face of one backplate clockwise until the wheel is locked, then loosen the adjuster by two or three flats until the wheel can be rotated freely.

Repeat the procedure on the remaining rear wheel, then check the handbrake adjustment as follows.

Apply the handbrake to the third notch. It should just be possible to rotate the rear wheels with heavy hand pressure.

To adjust the handbrake, loosen the cable locknut using a spanner through the access slot in the carpet behind the handbrake. Turn the adjusting nut until the correct tension is achieved, then tighten the locknut. Release the handbrake and check that the wheels rotate freely.

Before finishing with the handbrake, apply some lubricant to its cables and linkages.

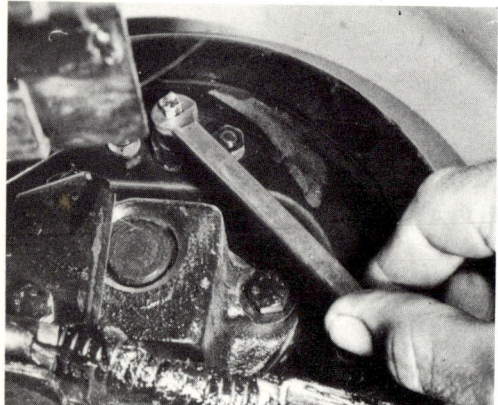

Adjusting the rear brakes using the correct type of spanner

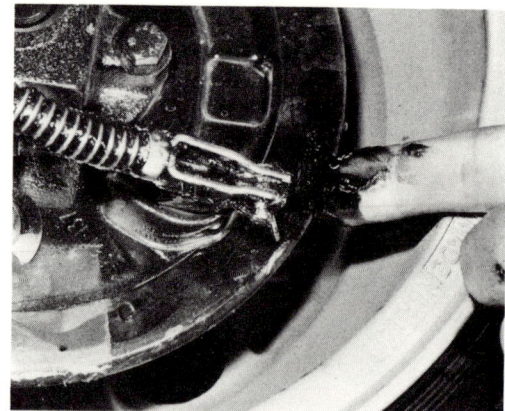

Lubricate the handbrake cable and linkages

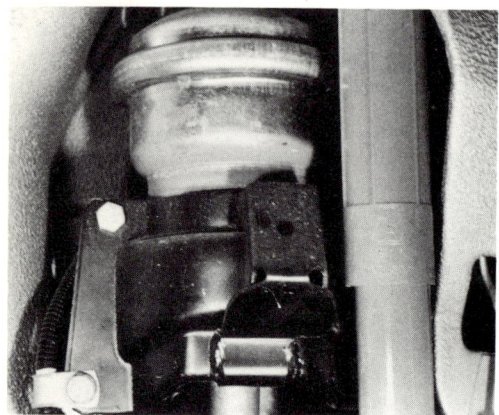

Check the suspension and damper units for signs of damage or leaks

A rear suspension pivot grease nipple

21 Rear suspension checks and lubrication

Make an inspection of the general condition of the rear suspension components, looking for signs of corrosion around the mountings, wear in the radius arm pivots and any signs of leakage from the Hydragas units. Any defective items must be reported to and repaired by your local BL dealer.

Lubricate the rear suspension pivot grease nipples, giving several strokes of the grease gun.

Remove the safety stands, refit the roadwheels, lower the vehicle and check that all tools are removed from underneath the car.

22 Check the headlight beam alignment

Although accurate headlight beam alignment checks and settings can only be carried out properly by a garage equipped with modern beam setting equipment, a general check and emergency adjustment can be made if necessary at this mileage interval. Proceed as follows.

Position the car on a level surface with tyres correctly inflated, approximately 10 metres (33 feet) in front of, and at right-angles to, a wall or garage door, then draw a horizontal line on the wall or door at headlamp centre height. Draw a vertical line corresponding to the centre-line of the car, then measure off a point either side of this, on the horizontal line, corresponding with the headlamp centres.

Switch on the main beam and check that the areas of maximum illumination coincide with the headlamp centre marks on the wall. If not, turn the plastic knobs located at the rear of the headlamps accordingly. Turn both knobs to raise or lower the beam and one knob (either will do) to move the beam horizontally.

23 Bodywork maintenance and checks

Thoroughly clean and polish the bodywork. Using a suitable length of stiff wire, probe the underside drain channels, the positions of which are shown in the accompanying illustration. Also check (where applicable) that the sunroof drain channels are clear.

Check that the windows operate freely. Also check that the seat belts are in good condition and the anchorage points secure.

Lubricate the door locks and hinges, also the tailgate and bonnet hinges and locks. Only light lubrication is required; any excess lubricant should be wiped off. Note that the steering lock must not be lubricated!

Lubricate the brake, clutch and throttle pedal pivots. Clear any debris from the heater air intake and drain.

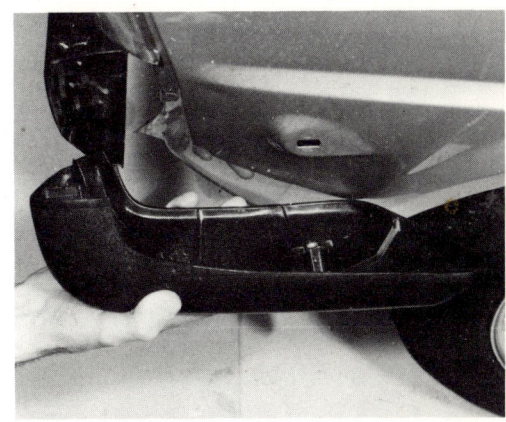

Access to the bodywork behind the bumper endpieces for cleaning

H16071

Drain holes (arrowed) must be inspected to ensure that they are not blocked. Those shown on the top of the car are for models fitted with a sunroof

H16073

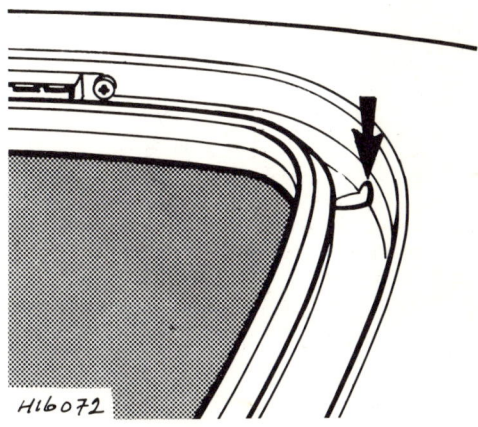

H16072

A sunroof drain channel

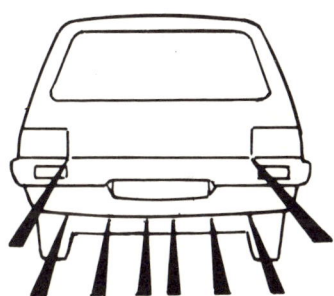

Drain channel points (arrowed) at the rear of the vehicle should also be checked

EVERY 18 000 MILES (30 000 KM) OR 18 MONTHS – WHICHEVER COMES FIRST

1 Renew the fluid in the braking circuit

The manufacturers recommend that the fluid be drained and renewed to maintain its efficiency. This is a task best entrusted to your BL dealer. For the more advanced DIY mechanic, the full details of this operation are given in the Haynes Owners Workshop Manual for the Metro.

One of the pressure bleeding kits available in DIY motor shops is an invaluable aid for this job. Follow the instructions supplied with the kit.

EVERY 24 000 MILES (40 000 KM) OR 24 MONTHS – WHICHEVER COMES FIRST

In addition to, or instead of, the items specified for the 12 000-mile service

1   Renew the engine oil filler cap

2   Drain and renew the engine coolant

It is preferable to drain the cooling system when the engine has cooled. If this is not possible, place a cloth over the expansion tank filler cap and turn it *slowly* in an anti-clockwise direction until the first stop is reached, then wait until all the pressure has been released.

Remove the filler cap, then position a suitable container beneath the left-hand side of the radiator. Loosen the clip and ease the bottom hose away from the radiator outlet. Drain the coolant into the container.

Place a second container beneath the cylinder block drain plug located on the rear right-hand side next to the clutch slave cylinder. Unscrew the plug and drain the coolant.

Before refilling the system with new anti-freeze solution, flush the cooling system to remove any sludge deposits. To do this, detach the top hose from the cylinder head outlet elbow, leaving the bottom hose disconnected also.

Insert a garden hose in the top hose, and allow water to circulate through the radiator until it runs clear from the outlet, then insert the hose in the expansion tank filler neck and allow water to run out of the cylinder head outlet elbow and bottom hose until clear.

Disconnect the heater inlet hose from the front of the cylinder head, insert the hose, and allow water to circulate through the heater and out through the bottom hose until clear. The heater must be turned on to 'hot'.

In severe cases of contamination, the system should be reverse flushed, necessitating the removal and inversion of the radiator so that water can be introduced through the bottom outlet. The engine will also probably require reverse flushing in this instance, in which case full details will be found in the Haynes Owners Workshop Manual for the Metro.

Reconnect the radiator, engine and heater hoses as applicable. Renew cracked or damaged hoses. Refit the cylinder block drain plug, ensuring that it is securely fitted. The coolant can now be poured into the expansion tank filler neck. Where new antifreeze mixture is to be used, add the antifreeze according to the manufacturer's recommendation for the degree of protection required.

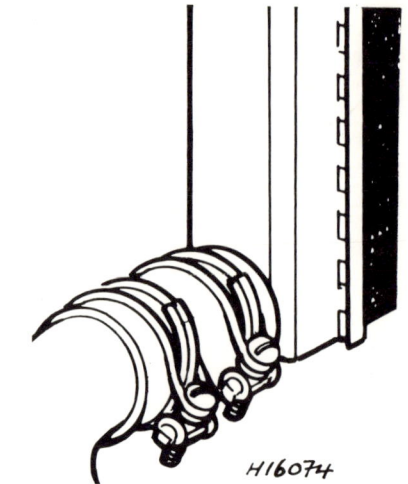

Detach the bottom hose to drain the radiator

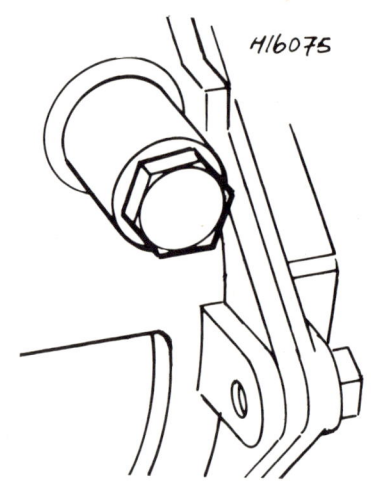

The cylinder block drain plug (at the rear of the engine)

Pour coolant into the expansion tank filler neck until it reaches the level mark, then refit the cap. Run the engine at a fast idling speed for three minutes, then stop the engine and check the level in the expansion tank. Top up the level as necessary, being careful to release pressure from the system before removing the filler cap if necessary.

3 Renew the distributor contact breaker points

Access to the internal components of the distributor, as you will no doubt have noticed, is not particularly good due to the close proximity of the radiator and the obstructing top cross panel. To simplify points renewal, some people advocate the removal either of the distributor itself, or of the top cross panel and radiator for better access. In our workshop, however, we found that it was possible to renew the contact breaker points with the distributor in position, but a certain amount of dexterity and care is necessary.

To start with we removed the top cross panel (bonnet lock platform), which is secured by cross-head screws. The bonnet will have to be supported in the raised position by some means other than the centre stay. With the securing screws removed, lift the panel clear and position it out of the way. For the complete removal of the cross panel you will also need to detach the bonnet release cable.

Unclip and detach the distributor cap and then pull the rotor arm off. The procedure now depends on the distributor type.

Lucas distributors

Press the moving contact spring from the insulator post and slide out the low tension connector. Unscrew the fixed contact retaining screw and remove the contact breaker set from the baseplate and pin.

Ducellier distributors

Remove the spring clip from the two pivot posts, then remove the fibre washer and lift the moving contact from the pivot post. Slide the LT wire retaining block from the distributor body and disconnect the condenser lead.

Remove the screw and washer and withdraw the fixed contact from the baseplate.

All distributors

The fitting and assembly of the new contact breaker points on both distributor types is a reversal of the removal procedure. On the Lucas version, ensure that the nylon plate engages the pin.

When assembly is complete, the contact breaker points gap must be adjusted as detailed in the 12 000-mile service checks. When this is completed refit the rotor arm and distributor cap, then relocate the cross panel to complete. Check and adjust the ignition timing if necessary.

4 Renew the alternator/water pump drivebelt

Refer to the 12 000-mile service checks for details of the removal, refitting and adjustment of this drivebelt.

The drivebelt is not an expensive item, and it is well worth renewing it at this mileage rather than have it break some rainy night!

EVERY 36 000 MILES (60 000 KM) OR 3 YEARS – WHICHEVER COMES FIRST

In addition to, or instead of, the work specified for the 12 000-mile and 18 000-mile services

1 Overhaul braking system

As well as renewing the brake fluid, have all rubber seals and hoses renewed at the same time. This is also a good opportunity to renew any damaged or corroded steel brake pipes.

This may seem like an expensive piece of preventative maintenance, but it's better than having a brake seal or hose fail in an emergency stop! In any case, it's not a job for the inexperienced mechanic. Study the Haynes Owners Workshop Manual for the Metro if you think you're up to it; otherwise leave it to your BL dealer.

SEASONAL SERVICING

If you carry out the procedures we've detailed so far, at more or less the prescribed intervals of mileage or time, then you'll have gone a long way towards getting the best out of your Metro in terms both of performance and long life. That's the good news. The other kind is that there are always other areas, not dealt with in regular servicing schedules, where neglect can spell trouble.

We reckon a bit of extra time spent on your car at the beginning and end of the winter will be well repaid in terms of peace of mind and prevention of trouble. The suggested attentions which follow have therefore been divided into Spring and Autumn sections – but there's nothing to prevent you doing them more frequently if you like!

SPRING

We've put this one first as it's less depressing than Autumn – though there's probably more work involved!

Underside of car

In Spring, we venture to suggest, the owner's fancy lightly turns to thoughts of cleaning off all the accumulated muck of winter from underneath the car. Without a shadow of doubt, the best time to clean underneath is the worst time from the discomfort point of view – that is, when the car's been driven in the wet and all the dirt's nicely softened up. So let's talk first about the easiest way out – steam cleaning or pressure washing. These are not DIY jobs, and can only be done at larger garages, usually those which undertake body repair jobs. You may feel this **73** method's unnecessarily expensive, but it's generally preferable to grovelling about underneath and getting filthy and uncomfortable doing it yourself. However, for the owner who really wants to do it by hand, here goes ...

You'll need paraffin or a water-soluble solvent, water (and preferably a hose), a wire brush, a scraper and a stiff bristle brush.

To start with, jack the car up as high as possible, preferably at one side or one end. For your own safety, support it on ramps or concrete/wooden blocks and chock the wheels which are on the ground. Unless all the wheels are raised, also apply the handbrake; and engage first or reverse gear.

Now get underneath (you've put it off as long as you can!) and cover the brake discs and calipers with polythene bags to stop mud and water getting into them. Next loosen any encrusted dirt and, working from one end or one side, scrape or brush it away. The paraffin or solvent can be used where there's oil contamination. After all the brushing and scraping, a final wash down with the hose will remove the last of the dirt and mud.

You can now check for leaks in the floor; if you find any, dry the area carefully, then use a mastic type sealer to plug the offending gap. Hollow sections of doors and bodywork can be sprayed or brush-painted with a rust-inhibitor to provide some extra protection. If there are signs of the underseal breaking away, this is a good opportunity to patch it up. Undersealing paint is available in spray cans or tins from accessory shops; one small point about putting the stuff on though, and that's to make sure the area is clean and dry, otherwise you're wasting your time.

While you're underneath, have a good look round for signs of rusting. Likely places are the body sills, floor panels and wings, and if you do find any rust have a word with the local BL man or body repair shop before things get too bad.

Bodywork

This too will have suffered from all the muck and salt that's around during the winter, and there's no better time to wash it thoroughly and check for stone chips and rust spots. You're bound to find some, despite the regular washing you've given the car — or meant to — throughout the winter. Treat as for rusty scratches (see *Body Beautiful*).

After the touch-up paint has thoroughly hardened, it's worth giving the car a good polish to prepare it for the long, hot summer ahead (well, there's no harm in hoping). If you're feeling really energetic you could do the interior as well (*Body*

Beautiful again) but the most important cleaning jobs are now done.

AUTUMN

With winter on the way, your car's electrical system is going to take much more of a beating than it has during the last few months. Now — and not on a dark night miles from anywhere in a snowstorm — is the time to check the vital components.

Lights

Check operation.

Renew any failed bulbs or check for faults as necessary.

Wipers/washers

These are going to get a lot of use, so check the wiper arms and blades. Top up the washer reservoir and check operation.

Radiator antifreeze mustn't be used in the screenwash system as it's harmful to paintwork. Special additives can be obtained for the screenwash reservoir to prevent freezing up during winter.

Cooling system

Check that the antifreeze solution in the engine cooling system's of the correct strength or, if there's no antifreeze in, add some. 'Bluecol' antifreeze or equivalent is recommended and can be left in the cooling system for up to two years. If you have antifreeze in already but are uncertain of its strength, it's advisable to have the specific gravity of the coolant checked by your garage.

Tyres

Check tread and condition. Remember that you may well be driving in slippery conditions.

Useful aerosols

When next at your local garage or accessory shop it's a good idea to get a can of ignition waterproofer, and you'll probably need a can of windscreen de-icer at your disposal sometime during the coming winter months. These items should be carried in the car so that they're always on hand when needed in damp or icy conditions.

Bodywork

Finally, if you've got any energy left, wash the car and polish it thoroughly to help protect the paint against the winter elements.

Body Beautiful

If you've bought this book intending to do all the routine servicing of your car yourself, then you'll surely want to keep the bodywork and inside of the car looking good too. For anyone who doesn't, here's how to do it anyway ...

Some people regard car cleaning as one of the joyful aspects of ownership, others look on it as a tedious task and a necessary evil. If you fall into the latter category, then the best plan of action is to do a little each week, dividing the job into sections. In this way you'll at least maintain a reasonable standard of appearance and break up the monotony of the job.

The really keen types won't only have the interior and bodywork dazzling, but will also keep the engine free of oil and dirt. Though you may be horrified at the idea, it's not a bad one when you think about it. For one thing, if you do carry out any repairs on the engine or surrounding components, the job will be made that much easier and more pleasant just because you'll keep yourself cleaner and be able to see what you're doing. Another point is that any oil or water leaks can easily be traced at an early stage and rectified before they get really serious.

It is not suggested that the car be thoroughly washed and cleaned from all angles every weekend by the average owner, but rather more on a seasonal basis, combined with (say) the Spring and Autumn service checks. Other than this, all that will be required will be a quick weekly wash and leather of the paintwork and a quick brushing-out of the interior.

It's always a good idea to clean the interior first; this way you won't get the dust all over your nicely polished exterior – or the car's! Begin by removing all the contents, not forgetting the odds and ends in the pockets and glovebox. Then take out all the mats and carpets, which should be shaken and brushed, or better still vacuum-cleaned. If they need further cleaning this can be done with a carpet shampoo, but let them dry thoroughly before you put them back. Any underfelt should be taken out and shaken, too, but don't try washing this or it may end up in rather more pieces than you started with.

If the carpets should just happen to be in such a bad state of decay that they don't merit cleaning, why not get yourself a decent set of replacements? You can get kits tailored for your particular model from specialist firms, and they're quite reasonably priced.

The inside of the car can now be cleaned with a brush and dustpan, or again preferably, a vacuum-cleaner. If the flex on the Hoover won't stretch to the car (and the car won't squeeze through the front door!) it might be worth thinking about investing in one of the small 12-volt hand vacuums which can be attached to your car battery – your accessory shop can probably show you one.

Seat and trim materials can be wiped over with warm water containing a little washing-up liquid, but for best results (particularly if they're very dirty) use one of the proprietary upholstery cleaners, which are specially made for the job. An old nail brush will help to remove ingrained marks, but don't splash too much water about and do wipe the surfaces dry afterwards with a clean cloth, leaving the windows open to speed up drying. The carpets can be put back when they're quite dry, making sure they're properly fitted around the controls etc.

You have to be careful about cleaning car windows, especially the windscreen, with some household products as these can leave a smeary film. Water containing a few drops of ammonia is probably best, but any stubborn marks and smears can be removed with methylated spirit; finish off with a chamois leather squeezed as dry as possible.

Just in case you should think that's it, there's still the luggage area to be dealt with. Take out that collection of junk that seems to have grown every time you open the tailgate, and get busy with brush or vacuum cleaner again. While you're at it, if you must carry all that stuff around, now's the time to try and stow it so it doesn't rattle any more!

Now you can pause for a moment – make a well-earned cup of tea perhaps – and take a critical look at the interior. Are there any nicks or tears in the seats or other trim? Is the headlining drooping or peeling? Some excellent products can now be obtained for repairs such as these. One of the most useful is probably the vinyl repair kit, which comes in various **75**

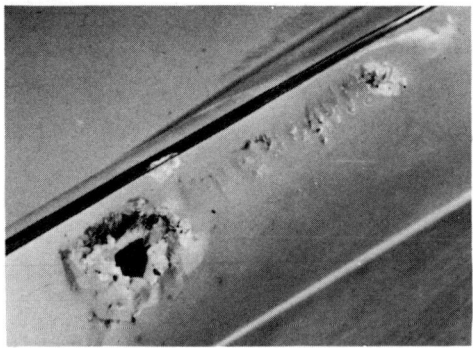

The procedure given with these photos is simplified; more comprehensive instructions will be found in the accompanying text. Typical rust damage is shown here, but the procedure for the repair of dents and gashes is similar.

First remove fittings from the immediate area and then remove loose rust and paint. A wire brush or abrasive disc mounted in a power drill is best, although the job can be done by hand. You need to be very thorough.

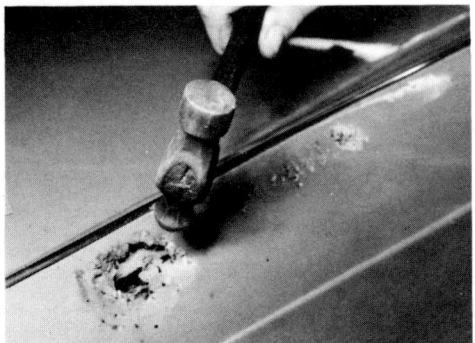

The edges of a hole should be tapped inwards with a hammer to provide a hollow for the filler. Having done this, apply rust inhibitor to the affected area (including the underside where possible) and allow this to dry thoroughly.

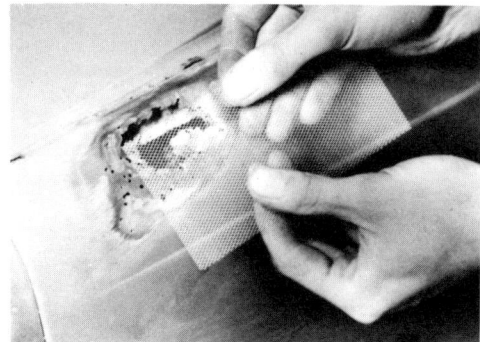

Before attempting to fill larger holes, block them off with suitable material. Metal tape can be used, but the picture shows a piece of aluminium gauze being sized up for use on this hole.

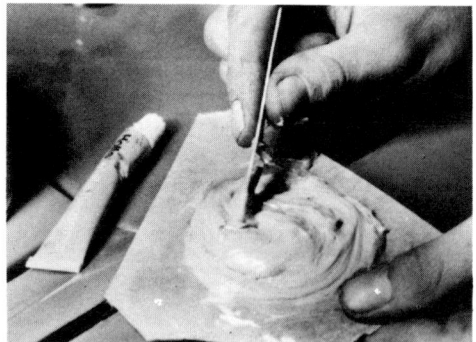

When mixing the body filler, follow the manufacturers' instructions very carefully. Mix thoroughly, don't mix too much at one go, and don't make it up until you're ready to start filling - modern fillers begin to harden very quickly!

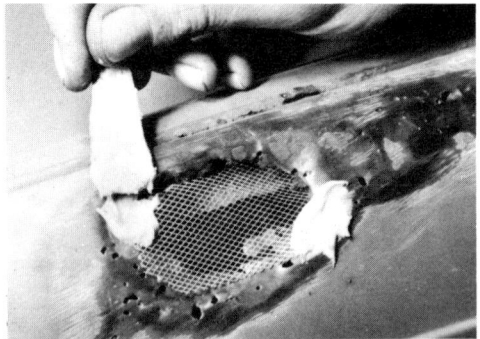

The tape or gauze used for backing up a hole can be secured in position with a few small blobs of filler paste. It's a good idea to mix a very small quantity for this purpose first.

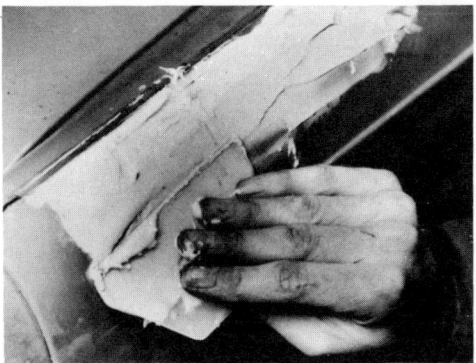

After mixing the filler, apply it quickly with a flexible applicator, following the contours of the body. The filler should be built up in successive thin layers, the final one being just above the level of the surrounding bodywork.

A fairly-coarse file or cutting tool is best for removing excess filler and for achieving the initial contour. Care must be taken not to overdo the filing or you'll hollow out the surface and have to fill it again!

A sanding block will now be needed; this can be made of wood as shown or a purpose-made rubber one can be purchased. Begin shaping the filler by using the block with progressively finer grades of dry abrasive paper, followed by ...

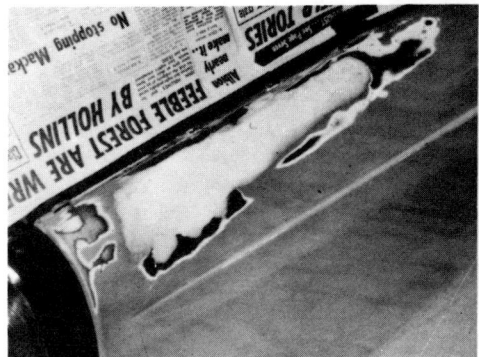

... wet and-dry paper, keeping both the work area and the paper wet. Rubbing down is complete when the filled area is 'feathered' into the surrounding painted areas, as shown; this final stage is achieved with the finest grade paper.

After thorough washing and drying, any necessary masking can be done and a coat of primer applied. Again, build this up with successive thin layers. Once the primer is dry it should be smoothed with very fine wet-and-dry paper.

The top coat of paint can now be applied, again in thin layers. Later a mild cutting paste can be used to blend it with the surrounding paint. Finish off with a good quality polish.

colours and consists of a quantity of 'liquid vinyl' and some sheets of texturing material. The liquid's applied to a split or hole in a plastic seat or piece of trim, smoothed like body filler, and allowed to set. It's then blended into the surrounding area by selecting the best matching pattern from the graining material supplied, placing this over the repair and rubbing with a hot iron; the pattern's then embossed into the repaired area.

For larger splits or tears it may be necessary to cut a piece of matching material from somewhere that doesn't show, apply some suitable adhesive to it and work it under the edges of the tear, pressing these together as neatly as possible once the glue has become tacky enough. Any loose headlining or trim can also be stuck in place – but make sure you get an adhesive that's suitable for PVC or vinyl.

The cropped nylon type of upholstery should be cleaned by brushing and then wiping over with a lightly dampened cloth.

Once you've got the seats in a reasonable state of cleanliness and repair, why not consider seat covers? Like carpets, they're available from specialist firms to suit your car and are a worthwhile buy in view of the protection they give.

If you use your car regularly and you've got the time and inclination, it should really be washed every week either by hand (preferably using a hosepipe) or by taking advantage of the local car-wash if there is one. Whichever method you choose (assuming you wash your car at all!) we don't think we need tell you how to do it – but remember it's never a good idea to just wipe over a very dirty car, whether wet or dry; you might as well sandpaper it!

Two or three times a year (even once is better than not at all) a good silicone or wax polish can be used on the paintwork. We don't know which of the many makes you'll use, so we can only recommend you to follow the makers' instructions closely so that you do see a reward for your efforts. Chrome parts are best cleaned with a special chrome cleaner; ordinary metal polish will attack the finish.

If the paint's beginning to lose its gloss or colour, and ordinary polishing doesn't seem to help, it will be worth considering the use of a polish with a mild 'cutting' action to remove what is, in effect, a surface layer of dead paint. Your friendly neighbourhood accessory shop man will advise on a suitable type.

The remainder of this Chapter describes how to keep your car's bodywork and paintwork in good condition by dealing with scratches and more major damage too, as they occur. A number of repair aids and materials are referred to, most of them essential if you're to achieve good results. They should all be available, together with free advice, from good motor accessory shops. Before repairing any paint or body-

work remember that the success of the work lies in the preparation.

Keeping paintwork up to scratch

With superficial scratches (the sort other people seem to get) where they don't penetrate down to the metal you'll be glad to hear that repair can be very simple. Lightly rub the area with a paintwork renovator or a fine cutting paste to remove any loose paint from the scratch and to clean off any polish. Rinse the area with plenty of clean water and allow to dry. Apply touch-up paint to the scratch using a fine brush, and continue to build up the paint by several applications, allowing each to dry, until it's level with the surrounding area. Allow the new paint at least two weeks to harden (knitting or a crossword puzzle will help to pass the time) then use the paint renovator or cutting paste again to blend it into the original. Now a good polish can be used.

When you've got a scratch that's penetrated right through to the metal, causing rusting, you need a different technique. Use your Scout knife to remove any loose rust from the bottom of the scratch, then paint on a rust-inhibiting paint to prevent it from spreading. You'll probably now need to apply cellulose body stopper paste – use a rubber or nylon applicator or a knife, but don't borrow one from the kitchen as you'll have a job cleaning it.

The paste can be thinned down if necessary using cellulose thinners. Before it happens, it's a good idea to wrap a piece of smooth cotton rag round the end of your finger, dip it in thinners and quickly sweep it across the filled scratch. This ensures that the area's very slightly hollowed and allows the paint to be built up to the correct level as described earlier.

Dealing with dents

When your car's bodywork gets a deep depression, you'll probably have one too. But there's no reason why even fairly large dents can't be tackled successfully by the DIY owner, especially using the excellent body repair materials now available. So cheer up, and let's see what can be done.

The first step is to try to pull the dented metal out to bring it more or less back to the original level. Don't expect to make a perfect job of this – you won't; the metal has stretched and 'work-hardened' which makes it a virtually impossible job. Try to bring the level up to about $\frac{1}{8}$ inch below the surrounding area; obviously, with shallow dents you can bypass this bit. If the underside of the dent can be got at, try hammering it out gently from behind, using a hammer with a wooden or plastic head. You'll need to hold a fairly heavy hardwood block on the outside of the dent; this absorbs the impact of the hammer blows and helps to stop the metal being dented in the opposite direction!

If you've got a dent in a completely enclosed body section, or there's something else preventing you from getting behind it, a different approach is needed. Try to screw up enough courage to drill several small holes through the metal in the dent, particularly in the deeper parts. Now screw in several self-tapping screws so that they get a good bite, and either pull on the heads with pliers or wrap some heavy gauge steel wire round them and pull this, Brace yourself in case something gives suddenly or you may dent your own bodywork!

Now to remove the paint from the damaged area. This is best done using a power drill and abrasive disc, but if you've got the time and energy you can use elbow-grease and abrasive paper. Don't forget to remove the paint from an inch or so of the surrounding good paintwork, too, so that everything blends in nicely. Now score the metal surface with a screwdriver or the tang of a file to provide a good key for the filler which you're going to have to apply. To finish off the repair, refer to the 'Filling and Spraying' section later on.

Rust holes and gashes

If there's any paint left on the affected area, remove it as described previously so that you can get a good idea of just how bad the problem is. If there's more rust or fresh air than good metal, now's the time to consider whether a replacement panel would be more appropriate; this is a body shop job, beyond the scope of this book.

If things don't seem that bad and you're prepared to have a go at doing the job yourself, remove all the fittings from the surrounding area except those which may help to give a good guide to what the shape should be (eg headlamp shells). Now, get a hacksaw blade or a pair of snips and cut out all the loose and badly affected metal. Hammer the edges inwards so that you've got a recessed area to build up on.

Wire brush the edges to remove any powdery rust, then paint over with a rust inhibitor; if you can get to the back, do the same to that. You're now going to fill the hole with something, but unfortunately just anything won't do. The best bets are zinc gauze or aluminium tape. The gauze is probably the favourite for a large hole. Cut a piece slightly larger than the hole to be filled, then position it in the hole so that its edges are below the level of the surrounding bodywork. If necessary, hold it in place with a few blobs of filler paste. For small or narrow holes you can use the aluminium tape which is sold by the roll. Pull off a piece of trim to the

approximate size and shape required. If there's backing paper, peel it off (it sticks better that way) and place the tape over the hole; if necessary, pieces can be overlapped at the edges. Burnish down the edges of the tape with a file handle or similar to make sure it's firmly adhering to the metal.

With the hole now blocked off, the affected area can be filled and sprayed as follows.

Filling and spraying

Many types of body filler are available, but generally speaking those proprietary kits which contain filler paste (or a filler powder and resin liquid) and a separate hardener are best. You'll also need a flexible plastic or nylon applicator (usually supplied) for putting the mixture on with. Mix up a little of the filler on a piece of board or plastic (those plastic margarine tubs are ideal but do wash out all traces of the contents first!). Read the instructions carefully and don't make up too much at one go. You'll find you have to work fairly fast or the mixture will begin to set, especially if you've been a bit generous with the hardener.

Apply the paste to the prepared hole or dent more or less to the correct level and contour, but don't try to shape it once it's become tacky or it'll pick up on the applicator. Layers should be built up at intervals until the final level's just proud of the surrounding bodywork.

When the filler's fully hardened, use a Surform plane or coarse file to remove the excess and obtain the final shape. Then follow with progressively finer grades of wet-or-dry abrasive paper starting with coarse, followed by medium, then fine (some manufacturers give 'grit' grade to their wet-or-dry paper — 40 is the coarsest, 400 the finest you will probably need). Always wrap the paper round a block if you're trying to get a flat surface, and keep it wet by rinsing in clean water, or the filler and paint will clog up the abrasive surface.

At this point, the doctored area should be surrounded by a ring of bare metal, encircled by a feathered edge of good paintwork. Rinse it with plenty of clean water to get rid of all the paint and filler dust, and allow it to dry completely.

If you're happy with the surface you've obtained then you're ready to apply some paint. First spray over the whole area with a light coat of grey primer. This will show up any surface imperfections which may need further treatment, and will also help you get the knack of spraying with an aerosol can before you start on the colour coats. Rub down the surface again, and if necessary use a little body stopper, as described for minor scratches, to fill any small imperfections. Repeat this spray-and-level procedure **79** until you're satisfied with the finish; then wash down again and allow to dry.

The next stage is to apply the finishing coats, but first a word or two about the techniques involved. Paint spraying should be done in a warm, dry, windless, dust-free atmosphere – conditions not very readily available to most of us! You may be able to approach them artificially if you've got a large indoor workshop, but if you have to work outside you'll need to pick the day carefully. If you're working in your garage you'll probably need to 'lay' the dust on the floor by damping it with water.

If the body repair's confined to a small patch, mask off the surrounding area to protect it from paint spray. Bodywork fitting (chrome strips, or door handles and the like) will need to be either masked or removed. If you're masking, use genuine masking tape and plenty of newspaper as necessary. Before starting to spray, shake the aerosol can thoroughly; then experiment on something (an old tin or similar will do – not the neighbours' car) until you feel you can apply the paint smoothly. At the previous stage this wasn't too important, but now you're trying to get the best possible finish.

First cover the repair area with a thick coat of primer – not as one coat, but built up of several thin ones. When this is dry, using the finest wet-or-dry paper, rub down the surface until it's really smooth. Use plenty of water to keep the surface clean; when it's dry, spray on another primer coat and repeat the procedure.

Now for the top coat. Again the idea's to build up the paint thickness by several thin coats. Have a test spray first as this is a different aerosol, then commence spraying in the centre of the repair area. Using a circular motion, work gradually outwards towards the edges until the whole of the repair and about two inches of the surrounding paint is covered. Remove all the masking material 10 to 15 minutes after you've finished spraying.

Now you can start putting away all the bits and pieces because it'll need about two weeks for the paint to harden completely. After this time, using a paint renovator or a very fine cutting paste, blend the edges of the new paint into the original. Finally, apply a good wax or silicone polish, and hopefully you'll have a repair which is only noticeable by its absence!

Adding 'Pinstripes'

There are various kinds of self-adhesive body decor available for customising your car, while some models of the Metro have their own side-stripes built in. Perhaps the neatest and most suitable of the 'add-on' variety are Pinstripes, and we've included these in this Chapter as they may appeal to the owner who wants a cheap and simple way to improve the appearance of his or her car. They're adhesive tapes which come in different widths and colours and as single or multi-stripes. Most have a backing paper which is peeled off as the stripe is applied.

When applying any of these self-adhesive tapes, first make sure the paintwork's clean by washing with warm water and a car shampoo or liquid detergent. Next clean up the surface with a very fine cutting paste or paintwork renovator, and wash down again. You can now apply the tape, but follow the directions carefully. Smooth it down with a clean rag and, if necessary, prick out any small air bubbles with a pin. Try not to stretch the stripes as you put them on because they'll shrink slightly anyway; and wrap the ends round the panels so that they don't pull away at the edges.

Upholstery painting

If you think the upholstery or interior panelling of your car requires renovating, or maybe you want to improve the colour scheme or make it look more sporty, there are various colours of upholstery paint available in accessory shops. You can also use the paint to cover up repairs, but make sure it's a perfect match or you could make things look worse.

The Personal Touch

On the subject of accessories it's been said that, if someone else makes it, the motorist will buy it. The 'after-market' in extras and accessories has now grown to enormous proportions, you only need to browse through a car magazine or motor accessory shop to see what we mean. The problem for any motorist is to sort out the useful and practical items from what, at the other end of the scale, is some undoubted rubbish.

The subject of accessories is so broad that in a Handbook like this we can only 'touch the top of the iceberg' so we've tried to cover just a few of the more popular accessories and to include some tips on fitting where appropriate.

All good products will be supplied with general fitting instructions which may or may not require minor modifications to suit your Metro. If you're buying secondhand, of course, you may get no instructions at all. The guidelines given here are in no way intended to replace the manufacturers' instructions, and if you're in doubt about fitting a particular item, they're the people to refer to.

Note: *Always disconnect the battery before commencing any work involving the electrical system.* Fireworks are very pretty, but there's a time and place for everything.

Auxiliary instruments

It would be possible to write a complete book on auxiliary instruments and how to fit them but, as with other things, you'll normally get pretty good instructions when you buy them. Because there are so many instruments available, we're only going to consider ammeters, battery condition indicators, clocks, oil pressure gauges, tachometers, vacuum gauges and water temperature gauges.

First of all, even before you've decided what instruments you're going to fit, you've got to think where to fit them. The dash panel of most Metro models doesn't lend itself readily to fitting brackets and small extra panels. On some versions there's room in the dash itself, but if you do decide to put anything there, make sure there's nothing immediately behind the mounting point because you'll have to drill and file out a suitable hole. Some instruments such as tachometers can be 'pod' types which are surface mounted. Another answer may be a central console, which will not only allow you to mount instruments but may have a radio installation compartment and/or a storage pocket. Some information on these is given later on.

Sooner or later you're going to have to start drilling some holes somewhere, but this needn't cause any real headaches if it's approached in the right way. As already mentioned, make sure there's nothing behind the panel before even considering drilling a hole, and that there's enough room to fit the instrument, switch, or whatever, in the space chosen. Any hole which will have a cable or capillary running through it must have a plastic or rubber grommet to prevent the metal chafing through; these grommets can be obtained from DIY accessory or car electrical shops.

When it comes to drilling larger holes for instruments, start off by centre-punching the middle of the area, then use compasses or dividers to mark the hole, allowing a little for clearance (standard instruments are 2 in/52 mm diameter). It's best to mark another hole inside the first hole, and drill around this line so that the centre part can readily be pushed out; if you're using a $\frac{1}{8}$ in drill the inner circle will need to be $\frac{1}{16}$ in inside the first circle marked. Finish the job off by carefully filing and deburring the hole.

An alternative method of cutting large holes is to use a tank cutter of the type used by plumbers. Some of these, which resemble a circular hacksaw blade, can be purchased in a variety of diameters and will fit in an electric drill, so removing much of the hard work.

Battery condition indicator

The battery condition indicator's simply a voltmeter, and as such must be connected to a good earth point on the body and to any suitable connection which is live when the ignition switch is ON. For convenience, this could be a wire attached to the ignition switch or fuse box. You don't need heavy cables for the battery condition indicator, 14/0.30 mm (14/.012 in) should be OK, but make sure the earth polarity's correct.

81

Some of the supplementary instruments and other accessories available from Smiths Industries

Clock

The 'up-range' models have a clock fitted when new, but owners of the downrange variants may wish to add a clock to their more basic model.

Clocks come in many forms, you can even get car clocks powered by dry cell batteries. Most car clocks which are wired to the car's power source contain semiconductors. If this means nothing else to you, it should mean that there's a negligible load on the battery and that the polarity's critical if you don't want to cause permanent damage. Connections are much the same as the battery condition indicator except that you don't want the clock to stop when the ignition's switched off. Therefore connect the feed wire to a fuse which is permanently live.

Tachometer

The tachometer (rev counter) is the one instrument that's available in larger sizes than the others (80 mm instead of 52 mm, although the smaller size can be obtained). Most are positive *or* negative earth, but you must connect them up correctly. In case you should pick up a secondhand one, connections for the most common types are shown in the illustrations. Note that with the Smiths type, the distributor-to-coil LT lead is removed; also note the sleeve colours on the main white lead. Use a 14/0.30 (14/.012) cable size.

Oil pressure gauge

Oil pressure gauges may have an electrical sender unit, similar in appearance to the water temperature gauge sender, or a capillary tube which carries a thin column of oil up to the gauge head. Either way, connection is made using a T-piece (usually supplied with the gauge) screwed into the oil pressure switch tapping, which is located just below No 4 spark plug. The existing warning light switch screws into one arm of the T, and the gauge sender or pipe union into the other arm.

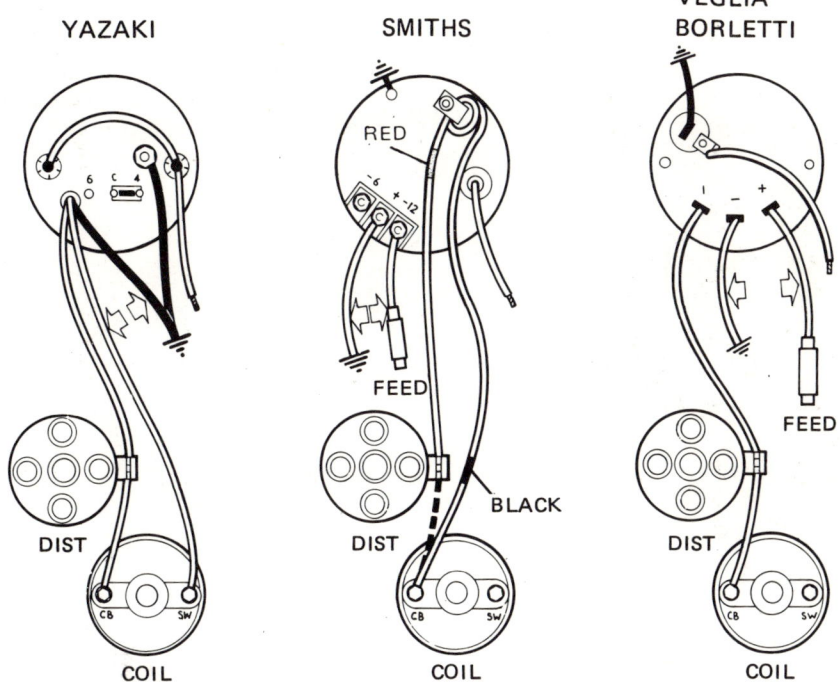

YAZAKI   SMITHS   VEGLIA BORLETTI

Connections for three popular tachometers
Yazaki: *Negative earth shown – reverse arrowed wires to change polarity*
Smiths: *Positive earth shown – the dotted connection must be removed when the tachometer is fitted.*
               Reverse arrowed wires to change polarity
Veglia Borletti: *Negative earth shown – reverse arrowed wires to change polarity*

With the electrical type of gauge, connections must be made to an ignition-controlled live point, to the instrument lighting circuit, and to earth, as well as to the sender unit itself. The mechanical type of gauge will only need the lighting and earth connections

The oil pressure switch location in the cylinder block

Vacuum gauge (performance gauge or fuel consumption gauge)

This is simply a suction (negative pressure) gauge which screws into a tapping on the inlet manifold, with a flexible pipe for the meter. Once you've got the hang of using it, it can be very useful as an aid to economical driving. The only tricky bit about installation is making a tapping point in the manifold. You may be able to use a T-piece in the brake servo vacuum line (if your Metro has a servo); otherwise, get advice from your local garage or from the place where you buy the gauge.

Consoles

Consoles come in all shapes, sizes and prices. Before buying, have a good look round to see what's on the market — that includes looking through the motoring DIY magazines. Some types extend back from the engine compartment wall or dash panel to behind the handbrake, the handbrake and gear levers coming up through the console base panel. You can get them with cut-outs for switches, radios and tape players, and for the standard 52 mm diameter circular instruments. Many types also have an ashtray or **83**

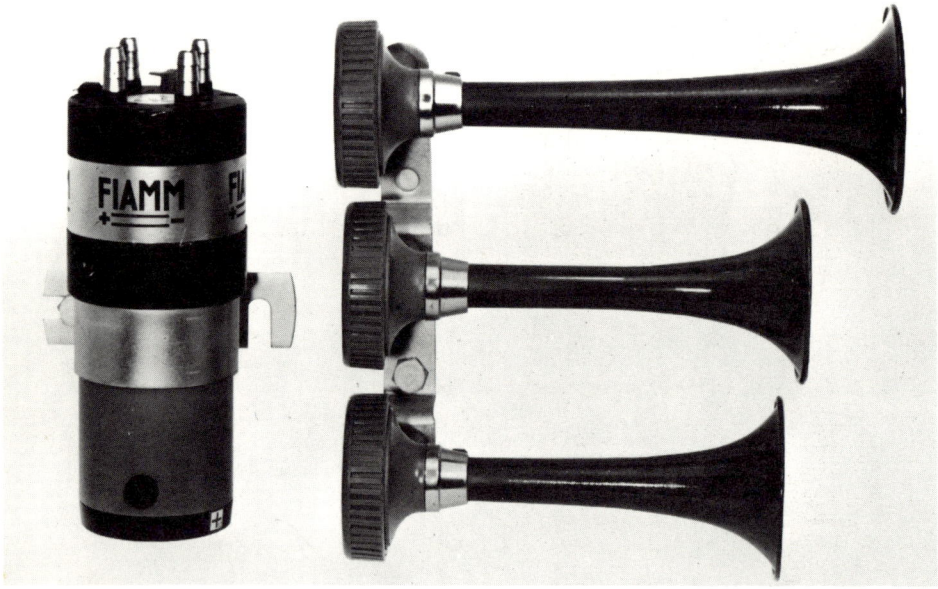

Fiamm 'Trio' air horns

storage pocket, some also have an arm-rest; there's even a type that fits to the roof! They come in a variety of finishes — black leatherette, fibreglass, or woodgrain, and in various colours. Without a great deal of difficulty you should be able to get something that suits both your taste and your pocket.

Fitting of consoles is usually straightforward, but you may need to drill a few holes which could lead to your buying some self-tapping screws as well. Before drilling, don't forget to look what's on the other side of the panel, or your 'extra' could prove extra expensive!

Warning devices
Air Horns

Air horns are marketed by several companies as a DIY installation kit comprising the horns themselves, a compressor unit, a relay, plastic piping and electrical cable. What you've obviously got to do is mount the horns reasonably near the compressor, and the compressor reasonably near the relay, or the connections just won't reach. It's normal for the manufacturers to specify a certain way up for the compressor to be mounted, but there shouldn't be any other problems. You'll need to make sure that the electrical connections are as per the maker's instructions for the relay and compressor, and decide whether you want to use the air horns in conjunction with, or in place of, the original car horn. If you have to connect into existing wiring, make sure the connections are

well made and, if these involve soldering, don't forget to insulate any soldered joints.

Child safety seats and harnesses

Much has been said in recent years about the use of seat belts for front seat passengers, and more recently there's been an increasing interest in the various special rear seats and harnesses now available for babies and younger children. It's not possible to give specific instructions for fitting these, because there are so many types around, but what you must be careful about is ensuring that you buy a BSI-approved type.

Most types have a pair of straps at the lower edge which need to be attached to the rear seat pan at the back of the squab, and a further pair of straps that fit over the back of the car seat for attachment to the floor or wheel arch. Take very careful note of the manufacturer's instructions; they require the anchorages to be a certain distance apart, and may also require reinforcing plates to be used. Before starting to drill holes for the mountings, make sure the underside or rear of the panel's clear of obstructions, pipes or any other components.

Lamps

When auxiliary lamps are fitted, not only must you fit them in a suitable place on the car, but you must also meet certain legal requirements; where these apply we've attempted to give some guidelines.

84

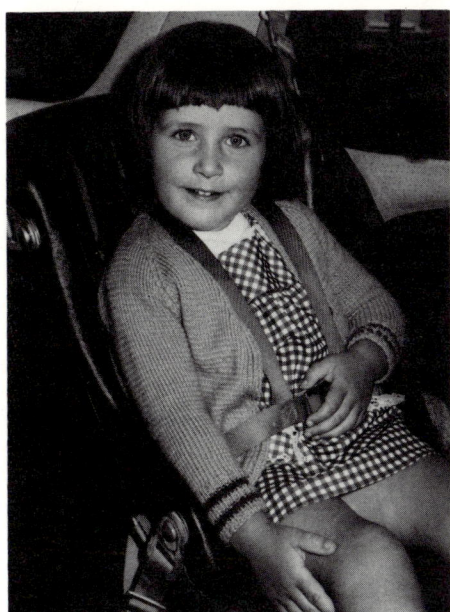

KL's Jeenay child safety seat

Spot and front fog lamps

It's illegal to mount these with the lower edge of the illuminating surface *more than* 1200 mm (47.24 in) from the ground. Any lamps that are mounted with this lower edge *less than* 500 mm (19.69 in) above the ground may only be used in fog or falling snow. In conditions where the law requires headlamps to be used, eg at night on an unlit road, a *single* lamp may be used only *in conjunction with* the headlamps. In these conditions the lamps must always be mounted and used *in pairs* (two fog, two spot or one of each) if they're to be used *independently* of the headlamps.

Their outer edges must be *within* 400 mm (15.75 in) of the edge of the car. If they're used as spotlamps, they should conform to the normal anti-dazzle requirements, eg by wiring them so that they go out when the headlamps are dipped, or by angling them slightly downwards.

Choose the lamps carefully, and if possible match the lamp styles. There are many good types on sale, so if you're not sure what you want ask for advice. The actual mounting is not too difficult; they can either be fitted to a bumper bracket or attached by a separate bracket to the front grille.

To prevent overloading of the existing wiring, a relay should be used (the Lucas 6RA type, part No 33213, is suitable). This is connected through the switch from the existing headlamp circuit to one of the relay 'coil' terminals, the other going to a good earth point. The lamp wires then go to one of the relay 'contact' terminals, with the other terminal being connected either to the battery or the battery connection at the starter solenoid, via a line fuse. The fuse rating will depend on the lamp manufacturers' recommendations, but will probably be about 20 amps for a pair of lamps.

Anti-theft devices

There are three main categories of car thieves — those people who want your car either as a complete item or for the major mechanical and body parts; those who are out for a joy-ride; and those who merely want the contents. With any type of thief it makes sense to do what you can to deter someone from *wanting* to get in; don't leave valuables lying about, don't leave the car unlocked and, if it's parked at home, put it in a locked garage if possible. But, if a car thief decides he does want your particular car, statistically he's got a pretty good chance of getting it!

All Metros have a steering column lock which is a very effective protection against a car being driven away, but it still makes sense to have a good burglar alarm fitted. Many types are available, and many of these are wired into door courtesy light switches or hidden switches beneath seats. Other types are wired into the horn circuit, but separate horns and bells are available; the more unconventional it is (whilst still being reliable!) the better. Don't put hidden switches in the first place you think of — it might be the first place the thief thinks of too!

Some anti-theft devices are activated by the movement caused through somebody trying to get into the car (and occasionally by an innocent passer-by!). Some not only sound alarms, but also earth the ignition circuit; other devices simply mechanically lock together the steering wheel and clutch pedal. Have a look round the accessory shops and see what suits your car, your pocket and the degree of protection required.

Radios and tape players

A radio or tape player's an expensive item to buy, and will only give its best performance if fitted properly. It's useless to expect concert hall performance from a unit that's suspended from the dash panel by string with its speaker resting on the back seat or parcel shelf! If you don't wish to do the installation yourself there are many in-car entertainment specialists who can do the fitting for you.

Make sure the unit purchased is the same polarity as the car (ie negative earth). Ensure that the units with adjustable polarity are correctly set before commencing installation.

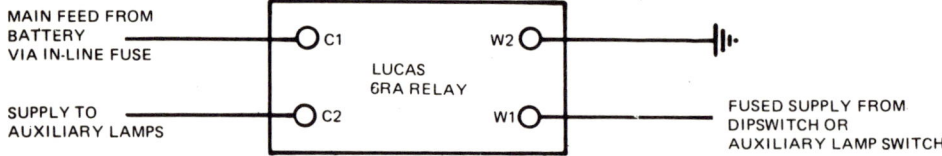

Connections for auxiliary lamps using a relay

It's difficult to give specific information with regard to fitting. In any case, the unit will come with its own instructions. However, the following paragraphs give guidelines to follow, which are relevant to all installations.

Radios

Most radios are a standardised size of 7 inches wide, by 2 inches deep – this ensures that they'll fit into the radio aperture provided.

The type of aerial, and where you're going to fit it, is a matter of personal preference. In general, the taller the aerial, the better the reception but there are limits to what's practicable. If you can, fit a fully retractable type – it saves an awful lot of problems with vandals and car wash equipment. When choosing a suitable spot for the aerial, remember the following points:

(a) The aerial should be as short as possible
(b) The aerial should be mounted as far away from the distributor and HT leads as possible
(c) The part of the aerial which protrudes beneath the mounting point mustn't foul the roadwheels, or anything else
(d) If possible the aerial should be positioned so that the lead doesn't have to be routed through the engine compartment
(e) The aerial should be mounted at a more-or-less vertical angle

Radio interference suppression

Books have been written on the subject, so we're not going to be able to tell you a lot in this small space. To reduce the possibility of your radio picking up unwanted interference, an in-line choke should be fitted in the feed wire and the set itself must be earthed really securely. The next step is to start connecting capacitors to reduce the amount of interference being generated by the different circuits of the car's electrics. The illustrations show the various interference generators and give capacitor values for the suppressors. When it comes to the ignition HT suppressors, these are resistors which can either be suppressor-type plug caps or in-line suppressors; if you're already using resistive HT leads (those with the carbon fibre filling), they're already doing the job for

you. They are standard equipment on new cars nowadays.

Tape players

Fitting instructions for both cartridge and cassette stereo tape players are the same and in general the same rules apply as when fitting a radio. Tape players aren't usually prone to electrical interference like radios – although it can occur – so positioning isn't so critical. If possible the player should be mounted on an even keel. Also, it must be possible for a driver wearing a seat belt to reach the unit in order to change or turn over tapes.

Visibility aids
Mirrors

Recent EEC legislation has done wonders for the looks of exterior mirrors. In addition to being functional, they now must have no projections to catch clothing or other cars, and must fold flat when struck. The result is a new wave of products in all shapes and sizes, some of which can be sprayed to match up wih the existing car finish.

All Metro models are fitted from new with at least a door mirror on the driver's side, whilst models such as the HLS are fitted with a mirror on each door. If you are thinking of changing the standard mirrors for any reason, choose mirrors which you think will suit the car's styling and, having got them, select the mounting point carefully. You'll get a good idea of where the best place is by simply looking at other cars, but get someone to hold the mirror while you sit in the driving seat just to make sure you can see all you need to.

Mark the position on the wing or door, and if you're fitting two mirrors do likewise on the other to make sure they're both in the same position. Check the hole size needed and, if you can, select a drill this size, plus, where applicable, a smaller one to make a pilot hole. If you haven't got the large drill required for most wing mirrors, you'll have to drill several small holes and file them out to the correct size.

Don't forget to remove any burrs from the hole afterwards, then paint on a little primer to cover the bare metal edges. When the primer's dry you can fit the mirror following the maker's instructions, then angle it as necessary to get the best rear view.

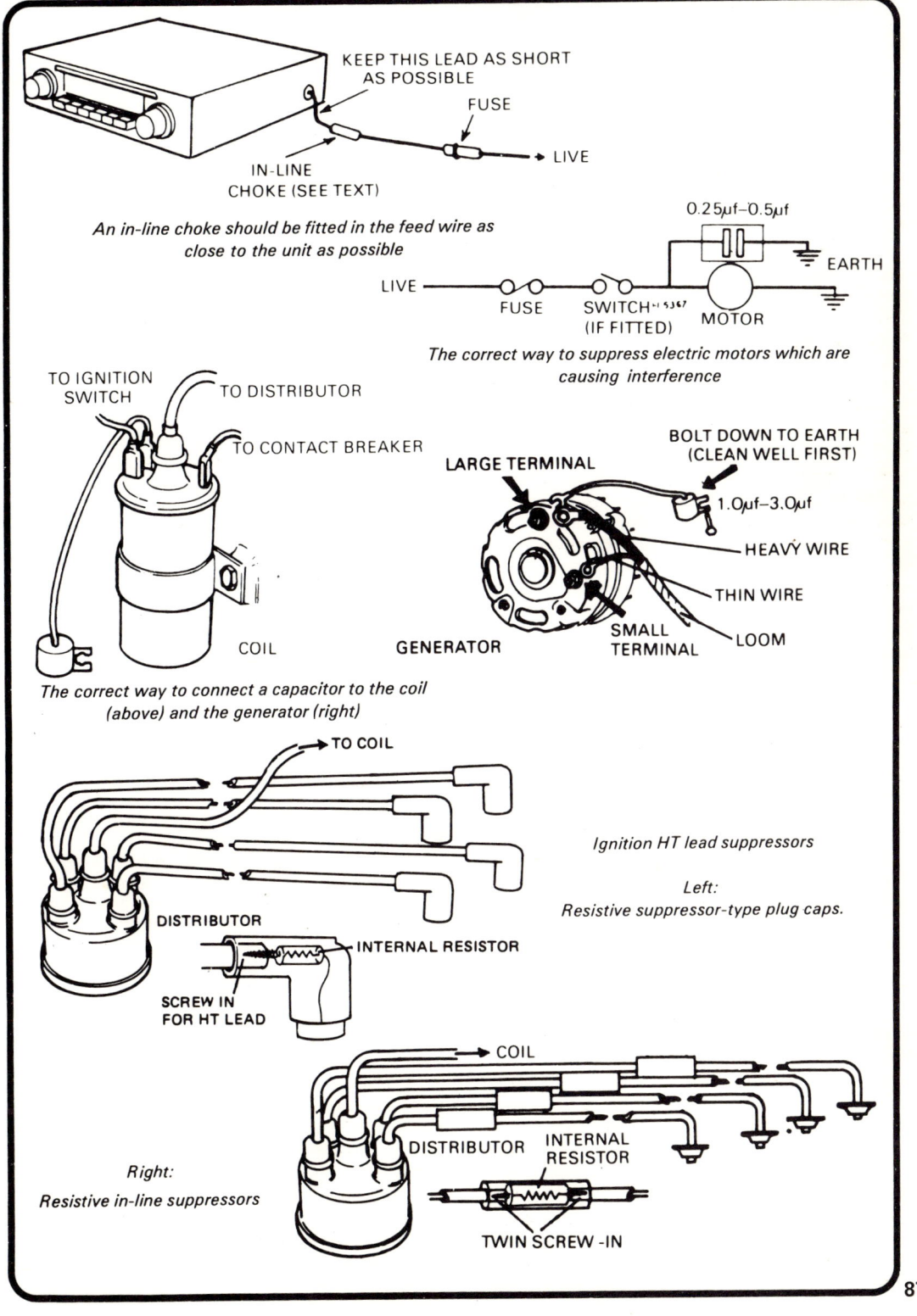

KEEP THIS LEAD AS SHORT AS POSSIBLE

FUSE

LIVE

IN-LINE CHOKE (SEE TEXT)

An in-line choke should be fitted in the feed wire as close to the unit as possible

0.25μf–0.5μf

EARTH

LIVE

FUSE

SWITCH (IF FITTED)

MOTOR

The correct way to suppress electric motors which are causing interference

TO IGNITION SWITCH

TO DISTRIBUTOR

TO CONTACT BREAKER

LARGE TERMINAL

BOLT DOWN TO EARTH (CLEAN WELL FIRST)

1.0μf–3.0μf

HEAVY WIRE

THIN WIRE

LOOM

SMALL TERMINAL

COIL

GENERATOR

The correct way to connect a capacitor to the coil (above) and the generator (right)

TO COIL

Ignition HT lead suppressors

Left:
Resistive suppressor-type plug caps.

DISTRIBUTOR

INTERNAL RESISTOR

SCREW IN FOR HT LEAD

COIL

DISTRIBUTOR

INTERNAL RESISTOR

Right:
Resistive in-line suppressors

TWIN SCREW -IN

Comfort

Longer journeys can be much more pleasant if your car's comfortable to drive, and just a couple of suggestions on this theme may be welcome.

Sound reducing kits

Very few cars have yet been produced in which the noise level, particularly at motorway speeds, is all that could be desired. For economy reasons, most manufacturers put only a certain amount of underfelt and sound-deadening material into their cars, and a further improvement can usually be made by fitting one of the proprietary kits. These are usually tailored to fit individual models, and consist of sections of felt-like material which are glued in place under carpets, inside hollow sections etc, in accordance with instructions. The material can also be bought in rolls for DIY cutting, using the carpets etc as templates.

Seats

If your car seats are showing signs of old age (and just fitting new covers won't disguise the sagging when you sit in them) then you can of course have them rebuilt by an upholstery specialist. On the other hand you could think about replacing at least the driver's seat by one of the special bucket types available. To look at these you'll have to find an accessory shop stocking the more motor sport orientated kind of goods.

Miscellaneous

Electronic ignition

Such systems are many and varied and widely advertised. The makers claim easier starting, better performance and lower fuel consumption as the main advantages, and on the whole these claims are substantiated in practice. However, before buying one of the available kits we suggest you stop and reflect whether your mileage and type of driving makes the expenditure worthwhile. Get other advice, preferably from someone who's fitted such a system to his own car. Consider too whether you're capable of installing it yourself, otherwise you'll have to pay for fitting as well.

There are several types of electronic ignition – some retain the conventional contact-breaker in the car's distributor while others replace this by a magnetic triggering device. Even where the contact points are retained they're no longer likely to burn and therefore shouldn't need replacing so frequently – but this doesn't in itself amount to much of a saving.

Steering wheels

One of the more popular, easily fitted accessories is a special steering wheel. Many types are available, but often it's also necessary to buy a boss which fits on to the steering column shaft, to which the steering wheel's then attached. No problems should be encountered when fitting a steering wheel or boss, once the old steering wheel has been taken off. To do this first set the front wheels to the straight-ahead position, then prise the cover free from the centre of the steering wheel. Unscrew and remove the retaining nut and mark the steering wheel and inner column relative to each other, just in case you should decide to refit the original wheel at a later date. The steering wheel can now be withdrawn. Don't try to hammer it off, you'll damage the column.

Roof racks

Many an owner has had to resort to a luggage rack from time to time, even if it's only for family holidays. The types available are very varied, but they normally rely on clips attached to the water drain channel above the doors. If you're buying, select a size that suits your requirements, making sure that it's not too wide for the roof!

When fitting the roof rack, position it squarely on the roof, preferably towards the front rather than the rear. After it's loaded, by the way, recheck the tension of the attachment bracket screws.

Do not overload the roof rack. Refer to *Vital Statistics* for the maximum allowable roof rack loading.

Don't keep the roof rack on when it's not wanted; it offers too much wind resistance and creates a surprising amount of noise (see *Save It!*).

Mudflaps

You're probably already aware that both front and rear wheel arches are fitted with mudflaps. These will not only protect your car's underside and paintwork from flying stones, but will also earn the thanks of following drivers owing to the reduction in spray during wet weather. Fitting's straightforward and is usually by means of clamping brackets or self-tapping screws.

Specialist fitments

We've now covered a lot of the main items likely to interest the average owner from the DIY fitting angle. Such things as towbars and sunshine or vinyl roofs, while practical or desirable, are beyond the scope both of this book and of the ordinary car owner. We therefore recommend that for any major accessory of this kind you consult the appropriate specialist who'll be able to give you an initial estimate of the cost as well as carrying out the work properly and safely.

Troubleshooting

We've gone to great lengths in this book to provide as much information on your car as we think you'll need for satisfactory running and servicing. Hopefully, you won't need to use this section but there's always a possibility (rather than a probability!) that something will go wrong, and by reference to the charts that follow you should be able to pinpoint the trouble even if you can't actually fix it yourself.

The charts are broken down into the main systems of the car, and where there's a fairly straight-forward remedy – the sort you can tackle yourself – **bold type** is used to highlight it. Further information on that particular item will normally be found elsewhere in the book; look up the particular component or system in the index to find the correct page. In some cases a reference number will be found (eg T1/1); by looking up this number in the accompanying cross-reference table, you'll find more information on that particular fault.

When confronted with a fault, try to think calmly and logically about the symptom(s), and you'll soon be able to work out what the fault *can't* be! Check or substitute one item at a time, otherwise when you do clear the fault you may not know exactly what was causing it. The commonest cause of difficulty in starting, especially in winter, is a poor spark at the plugs combined with a slow cranking speed from the starter motor. Make sure that your battery's kept fully charged, that the HT leads, coil and distributor cap are clean and dry, that the contact breaker points are in good condition and correctly gapped, and that all connections are clean and tight. If all this is in order, then proceed with fault finding in other areas.

TROUBLESHOOTER 1:

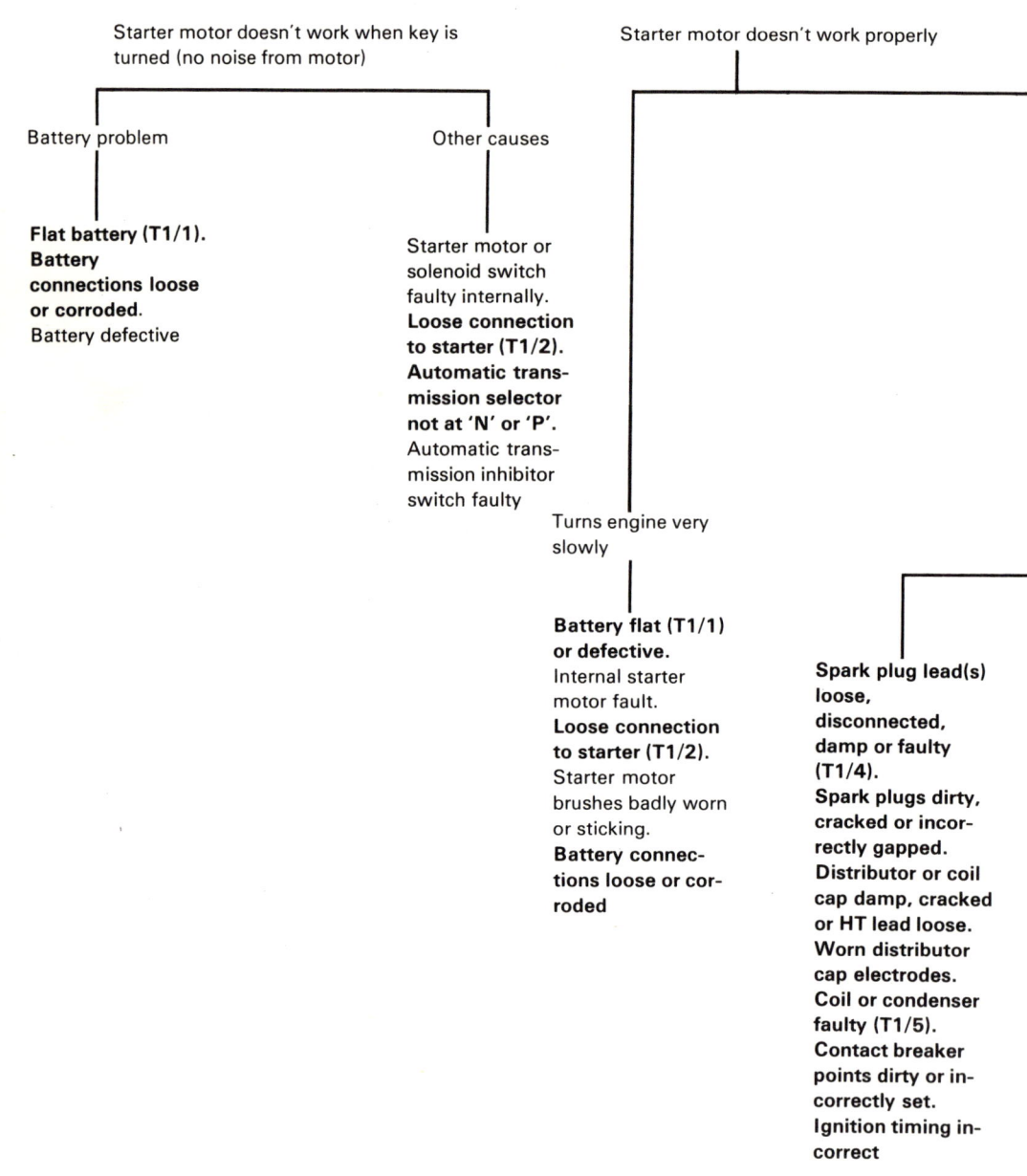

Starter motor doesn't work when key is turned (no noise from motor)

Starter motor doesn't work properly

Battery problem

Other causes

**Flat battery (T1/1).
Battery
connections loose
or corroded.**
Battery defective

Starter motor or
solenoid switch
faulty internally.
**Loose connection
to starter (T1/2).
Automatic trans-
mission selector
not at 'N' or 'P'.**
Automatic trans-
mission inhibitor
switch faulty

Turns engine very
slowly

**Battery flat (T1/1)
or defective.**
Internal starter
motor fault.
**Loose connection
to starter (T1/2).**
Starter motor
brushes badly worn
or sticking.
**Battery connec-
tions loose or cor-
roded**

**Spark plug lead(s)
loose,
disconnected,
damp or faulty
(T1/4).
Spark plugs dirty,
cracked or incor-
rectly gapped.
Distributor or coil
cap damp, cracked
or HT lead loose.
Worn distributor
cap electrodes.
Coil or condenser
faulty (T1/5).
Contact breaker
points dirty or in-
correctly set.
Ignition timing in-
correct**

ENGINE – STARTING

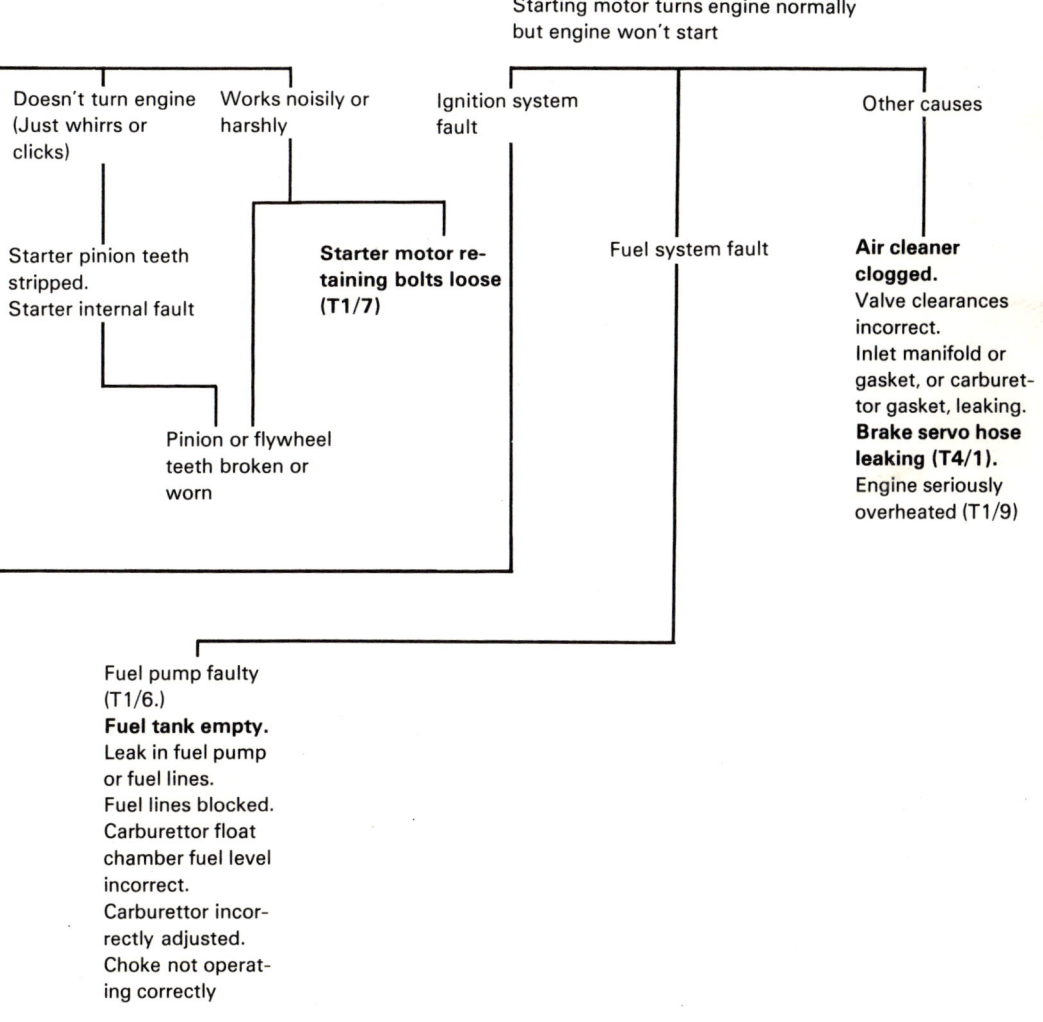

Starting motor turns engine normally but engine won't start

Doesn't turn engine (Just whirrs or clicks)

Works noisily or harshly

Ignition system fault

Other causes

Starter pinion teeth stripped.
Starter internal fault

Starter motor re-
taining bolts loose
(T1/7)

Fuel system fault

Air cleaner
clogged.
Valve clearances
incorrect.
Inlet manifold or
gasket, or carburet-
tor gasket, leaking.
Brake servo hose
leaking (T4/1).
Engine seriously
overheated (T1/9)

Pinion or flywheel
teeth broken or
worn

Fuel pump faulty
(T1/6.)
Fuel tank empty.
Leak in fuel pump
or fuel lines.
Fuel lines blocked.
Carburettor float
chamber fuel level
incorrect.
Carburettor incor-
rectly adjusted.
Choke not operat-
ing correctly

TROUBLESHOOTER 2:

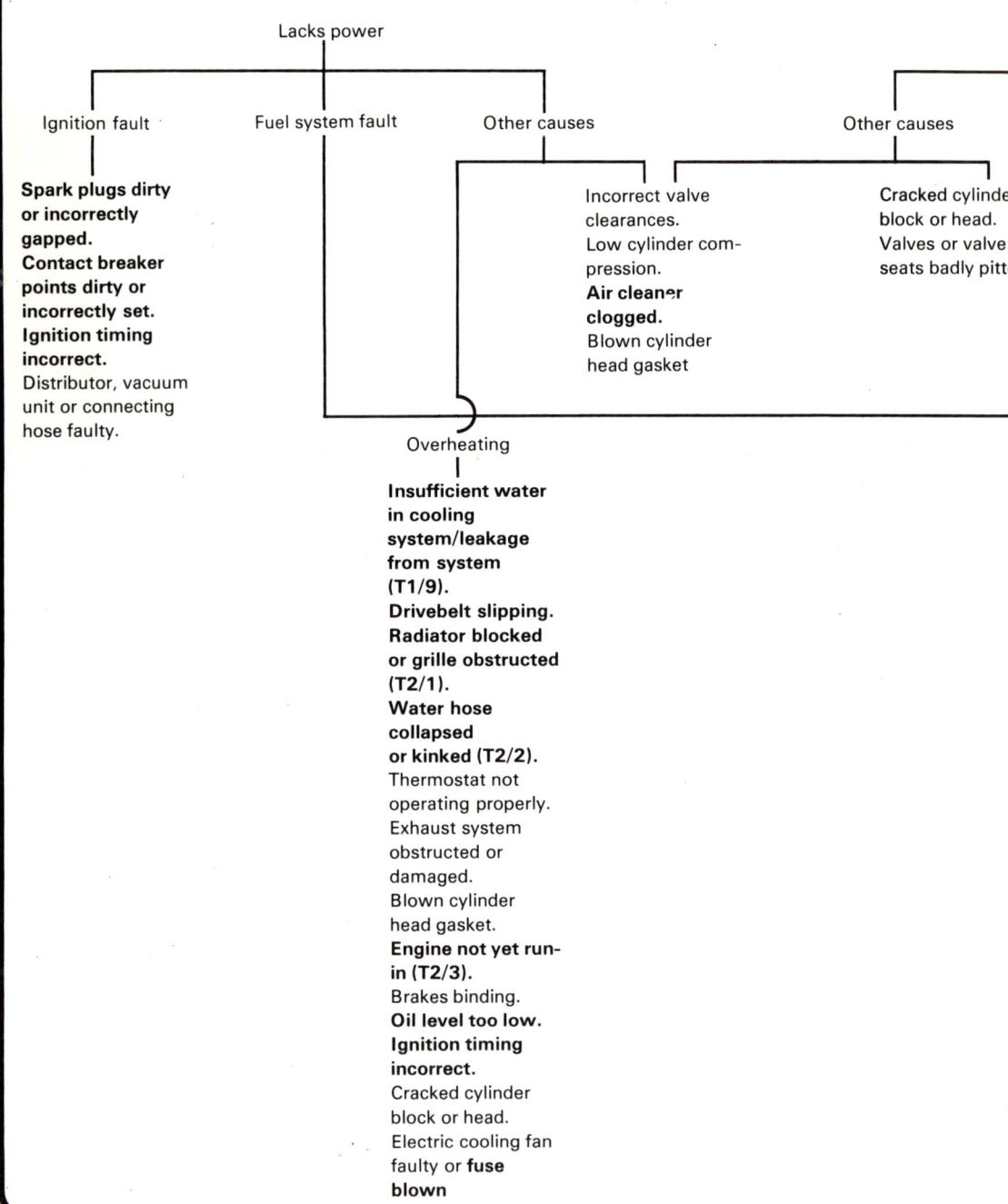

Lacks power

Ignition fault

**Spark plugs dirty
or incorrectly
gapped.
Contact breaker
points dirty or
incorrectly set.
Ignition timing
incorrect.**
Distributor, vacuum
unit or connecting
hose faulty.

Fuel system fault

Other causes

Incorrect valve
clearances.
Low cylinder com-
pression.
**Air cleaner
clogged.**
Blown cylinder
head gasket

Other causes

Cracked cylinder
block or head.
Valves or valve
seats badly pitted

Overheating

**Insufficient water
in cooling
system/leakage
from system
(T1/9).
Drivebelt slipping.
Radiator blocked
or grille obstructed
(T2/1).
Water hose
collapsed
or kinked (T2/2).**
Thermostat not
operating properly.
Exhaust system
obstructed or
damaged.
Blown cylinder
head gasket.
**Engine not yet run-
in (T2/3).**
Brakes binding.
**Oil level too low.
Ignition timing
incorrect.**
Cracked cylinder
block or head.
Electric cooling fan
faulty or **fuse
blown**

ENGINE – RUNNING

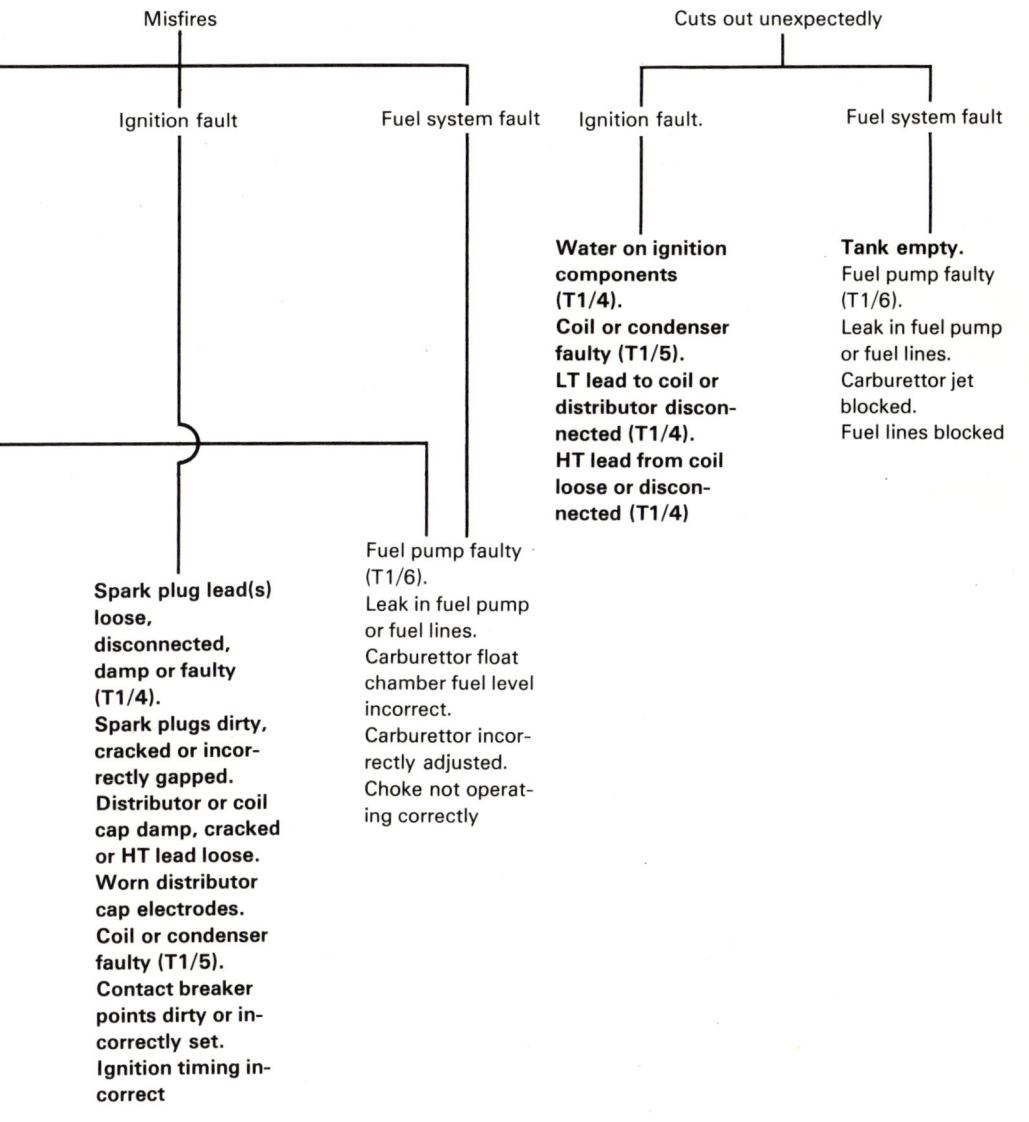

Misfires

Ignition fault

Fuel system fault

Cuts out unexpectedly

Ignition fault.

Fuel system fault

**Water on ignition
components
(T1/4).
Coil or condenser
faulty (T1/5).
LT lead to coil or
distributor discon-
nected (T1/4).
HT lead from coil
loose or discon-
nected (T1/4)**

Tank empty.
Fuel pump faulty
(T1/6).
Leak in fuel pump
or fuel lines.
Carburettor jet
blocked.
Fuel lines blocked

Fuel pump faulty
(T1/6).
Leak in fuel pump
or fuel lines.
Carburettor float
chamber fuel level
incorrect.
Carburettor incor-
rectly adjusted.
Choke not operat-
ing correctly

**Spark plug lead(s)
loose,
disconnected,
damp or faulty
(T1/4).
Spark plugs dirty,
cracked or incor-
rectly gapped.
Distributor or coil
cap damp, cracked
or HT lead loose.
Worn distributor
cap electrodes.
Coil or condenser
faulty (T1/5).
Contact breaker
points dirty or in-
correctly set.
Ignition timing in-
correct**

TROUBLESHOOTER 3:

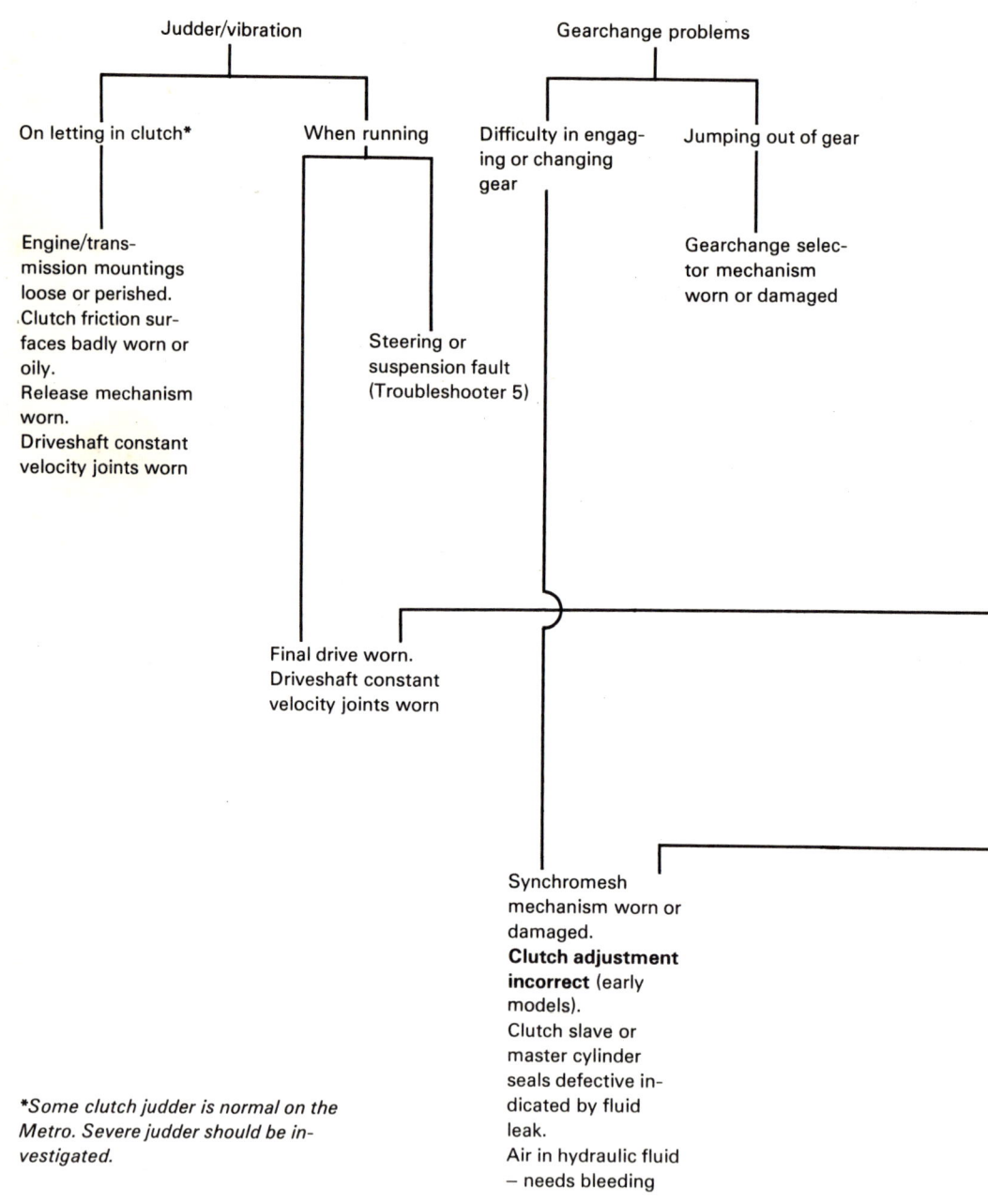

Judder/vibration

Gearchange problems

On letting in clutch*

When running

Difficulty in engaging or changing gear

Jumping out of gear

Engine/transmission mountings loose or perished.
Clutch friction surfaces badly worn or oily.
Release mechanism worn.
Driveshaft constant velocity joints worn

Steering or suspension fault (Troubleshooter 5)

Gearchange selector mechanism worn or damaged

Final drive worn.
Driveshaft constant velocity joints worn

Synchromesh mechanism worn or damaged.
Clutch adjustment incorrect (early models).
Clutch slave or master cylinder seals defective indicated by fluid leak.
Air in hydraulic fluid – needs bleeding

*Some clutch judder is normal on the Metro. Severe judder should be investigated.

CLUTCH, GEARBOX AND FINAL DRIVE

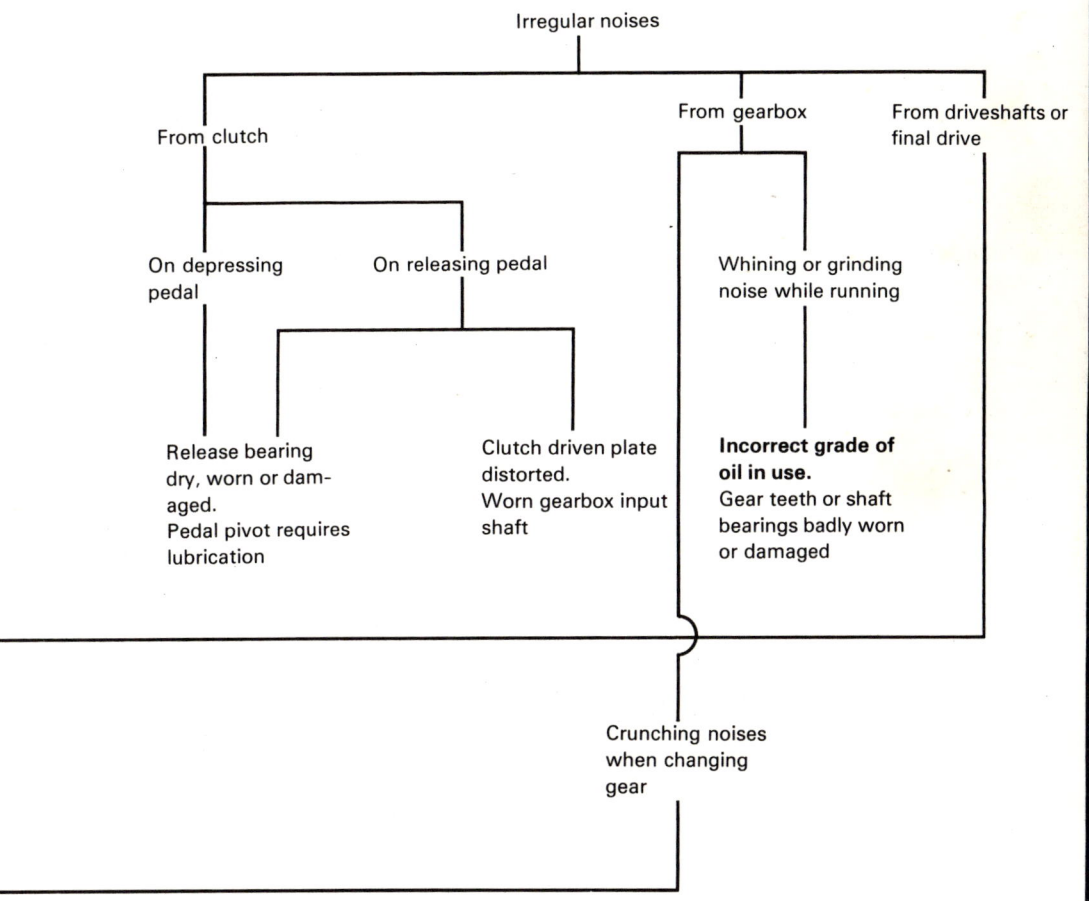

Irregular noises

From clutch

From gearbox

From driveshafts or final drive

On depressing pedal

On releasing pedal

Whining or grinding noise while running

Release bearing dry, worn or damaged.
Pedal pivot requires lubrication

Clutch driven plate distorted.
Worn gearbox input shaft

Incorrect grade of oil in use.
Gear teeth or shaft bearings badly worn or damaged

Crunching noises when changing gear

NOTE: Owing to the complexity of an automatic transmission unit, any fault diagnosis should be entrusted to your local dealer, who will have the necessary specialised equipment to test the unit.

TROUBLESHOOTER 4:

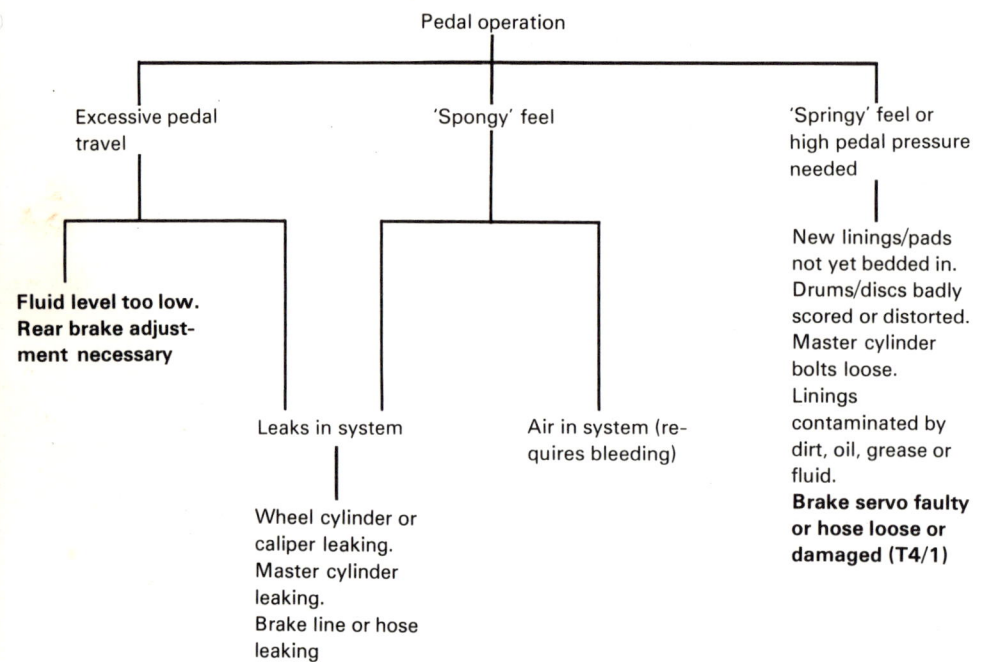

Pedal operation

Excessive pedal travel

Fluid level too low. Rear brake adjustment necessary

'Spongy' feel

Leaks in system

Wheel cylinder or caliper leaking. Master cylinder leaking. Brake line or hose leaking

Air in system (requires bleeding)

'Springy' feel or high pedal pressure needed

New linings/pads not yet bedded in. Drums/discs badly scored or distorted. Master cylinder bolts loose. Linings contaminated by dirt, oil, grease or fluid. **Brake servo faulty or hose loose or damaged (T4/1)**

TROUBLESHOOTER 5:

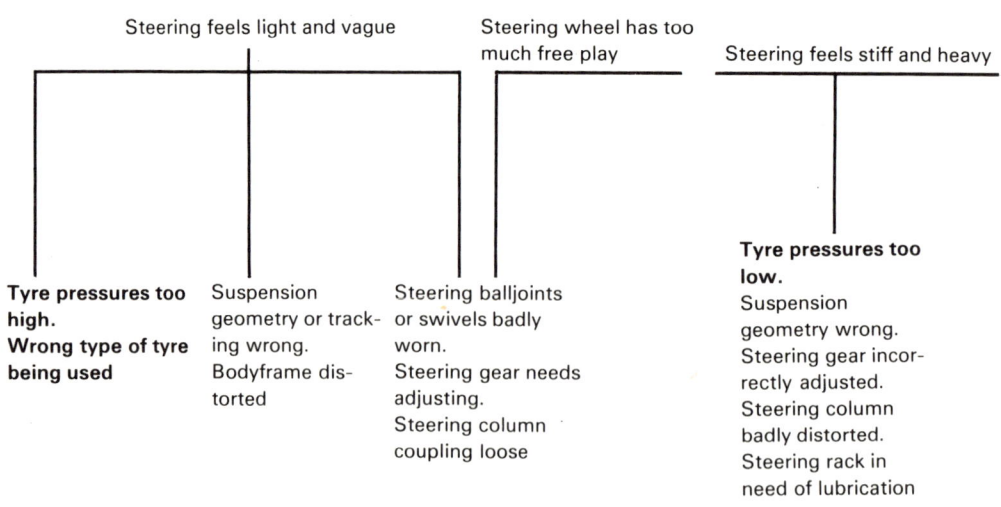

Steering feels light and vague

Steering wheel has too much free play

Steering feels stiff and heavy

Tyre pressures too high. Wrong type of tyre being used

Suspension geometry or tracking wrong. Bodyframe distorted

Steering balljoints or swivels badly worn. Steering gear needs adjusting. Steering column coupling loose

Tyre pressures too low. Suspension geometry wrong. Steering gear incorrectly adjusted. Steering column badly distorted. Steering rack in need of lubrication

BRAKES

Effect on car

Car pulls to one side	Brakes 'grab' or wheel(s) lock	Brakes bind when pedal released
Tyre pressures un-equal. Drums/linings or pads/discs contaminated with oil, grease or fluid. Brake backplate, caliper or disc loose. **Shoes or pads incorrectly fitted. Differing types of linings fitted at each side.** Suspension anchorages loose. Drums/discs badly worn or distorted	Contamination by dirt, oil, grease or fluid	**Handbrake over-adjusted.** Master cylinder pushrod out of adjustment. **Vent hole in reservoir cap blocked.** Master cylinder or wheel cylinder seized. **Broken or weak brake shoe return springs on rear brakes**

STEERING/SUSPENSION

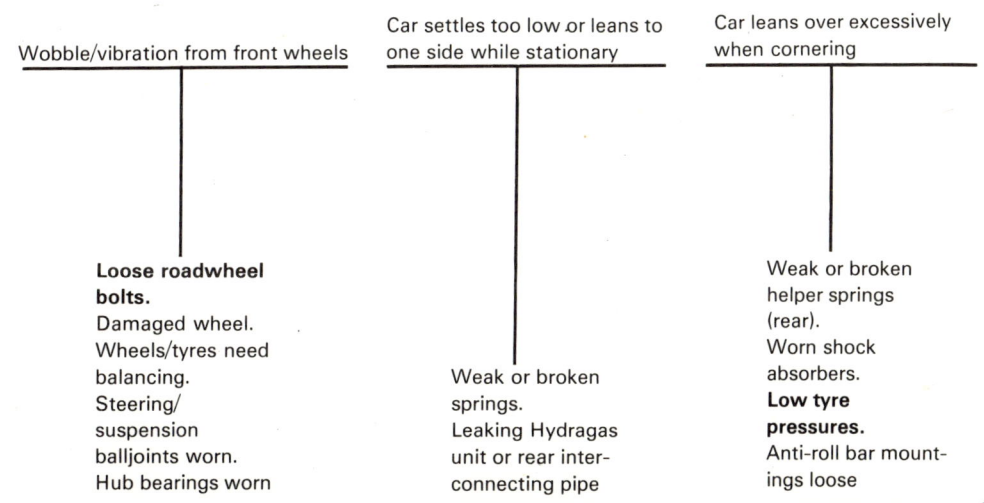

Wobble/vibration from front wheels	Car settles too low or leans to one side while stationary	Car leans over excessively when cornering
Loose roadwheel bolts. Damaged wheel. Wheels/tyres need balancing. Steering/suspension balljoints worn. Hub bearings worn	Weak or broken springs. Leaking Hydragas unit or rear interconnecting pipe	Weak or broken helper springs (rear). Worn shock absorbers. **Low tyre pressures.** Anti-roll bar mountings loose

TROUBLESHOOTER 6:

NOTE: This chart assumes that the battery installed in your car is in good condition and is of the correct specification, and that the terminal connections are clean and tight. A car used frequently for stop-start motoring or for short journeys (particularly in winter when lights, heater blower etc are likely to be in use) may need its battery recharged at intervals to keep it serviceable. If an electrical problem occurs, don't immediately suspect the starter or any other component without first checking that the battery is capable of supplying its demands.

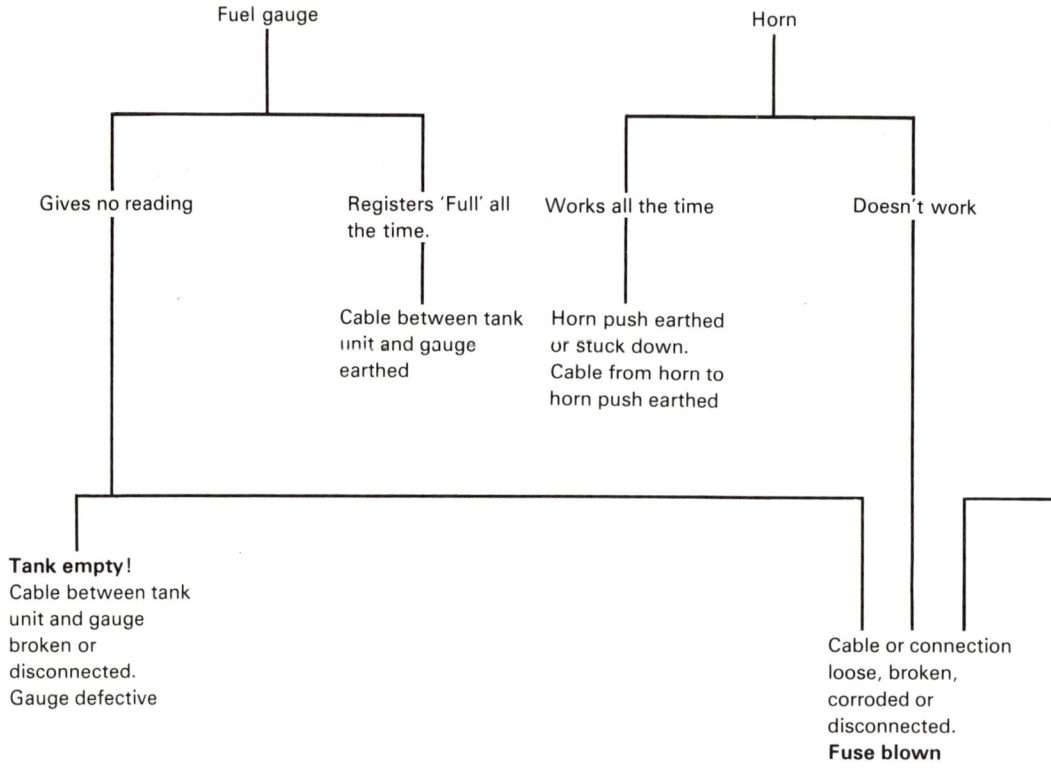

Fuel gauge

Horn

Gives no reading

Registers 'Full' all the time.

Works all the time

Doesn't work

Cable between tank unit and gauge earthed

Horn push earthed or stuck down. Cable from horn to horn push earthed

Tank empty!
Cable between tank unit and gauge broken or disconnected.
Gauge defective

Cable or connection loose, broken, corroded or disconnected.
Fuse blown

A fault occurring in any other electrical equipment or accessory not specifically referred to can usually be traced to one of the three main causes, ie blown fuse; loose or broken connection to power supply or earth; or internal fault in the component concerned.

ELECTRICS

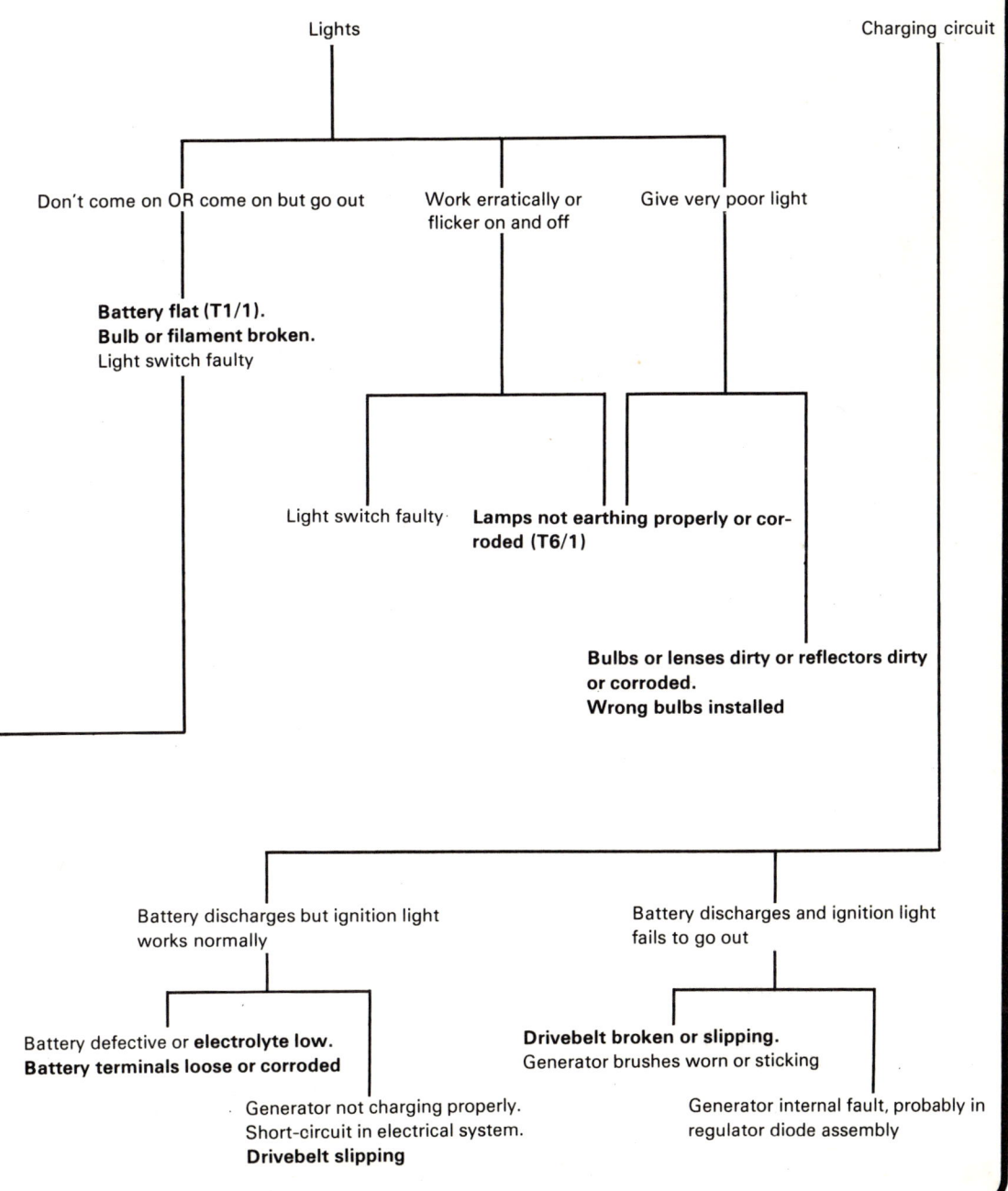

Lights

Charging circuit

Don't come on OR come on but go out

Work erratically or flicker on and off

Give very poor light

Battery flat (T1/1).
Bulb or filament broken.
Light switch faulty

Light switch faulty

**Lamps not earthing properly or cor-
roded (T6/1)**

**Bulbs or lenses dirty or reflectors dirty
or corroded.**
Wrong bulbs installed

Battery discharges but ignition light
works normally

Battery discharges and ignition light
fails to go out

Battery defective or **electrolyte low.**
Battery terminals loose or corroded

Drivebelt broken or slipping.
Generator brushes worn or sticking

Generator not charging properly.
Short-circuit in electrical system.
Drivebelt slipping

Generator internal fault, probably in
regulator diode assembly

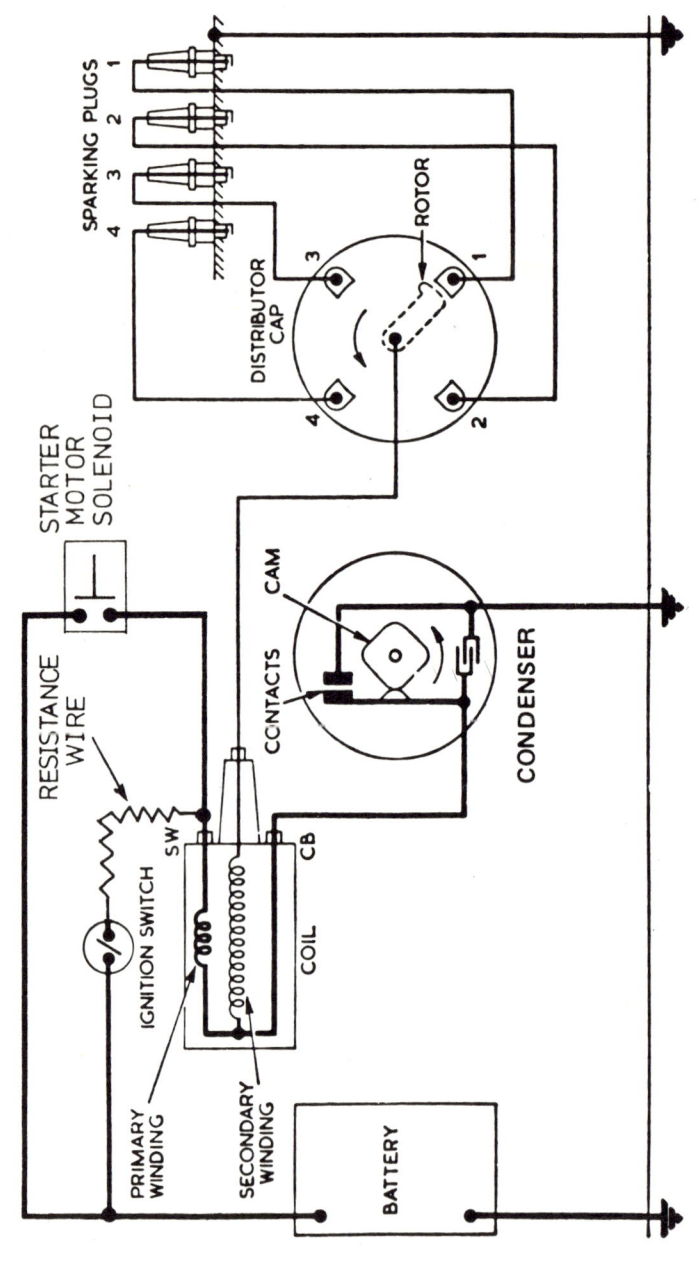

SPARKING PLUGS

1
2
3
4

ROTOR

DISTRIBUTOR CAP

3

1

4

2

STARTER MOTOR SOLENOID

RESISTANCE WIRE

IGNITION SWITCH

SW

CB

COIL

PRIMARY WINDING

SECONDARY WINDING

CONTACTS

CAM

CONDENSER

BATTERY

Ignition system simplified circuit diagram. The primary (LT) circuit is shown by heavier lines. Note that the resistance wire to the coil is bypassed when the starter motor is operating

CROSS-REFERENCE TABLE

TROUBLESHOOTER REFERENCE	ADDITIONAL INFORMATION

T1/1 Either charge the battery from a battery charger, or use jump leads to start the car from another battery; make sure that the lead polarities are correct in both cases or you may do permanent damage.

T1/2 If the lead's loose, disconnect the battery earth lead, then tighten the connection on the starter motor. Reconnect the battery earth lead.

T1/3 Select 3rd gear (manual models only) and have a friend give you a push. As soon as you gather speed, let in the clutch. Drive to your dealer for (possibly) a new starter motor.

T1/4 Make sure all the connections are tight, then wipe the leads clean and dry with a lint-free cloth. Use an ignition system waterproofer (eg WD40 or Damp Start) to prevent it happening again if this is a regular problem with your car.

T1/5 An ignition coil or condenser is a simple item to fit, but make a note of the connections before removing them, and ensure that the replacement coil is the correct type.

T1/6 To check the operation of the pump, detach the fuel outlet pipe (that's the one that goes to the carburettor) and operate it by turning the engine over on the starter a few times. There should be a steady stream of petrol in spurts if the pump's working properly. Take care you don't spill fuel on the hot exhaust!

T1/7 It's easy enough to tighten the attachment bolts if you've got a box or socket spanner of the right size.

T1/8 For a temporary repair a leaking water hose can normally be bound up with adhesive tape or, better still, with a hose bandage specially made for this purpose.

T1/9 Wait till the system's cooled down, then top it up. If it happens a second time, get it looked at straight away or you could ruin your engine (if it hasn't happened already). If it's just a leaking water hose you can probably bind it up as in T1/8 (above) to get yourself home.

T2/1 Driving carefully will probably get you home. An air line on the radiator core will clean out the dirt that's accumulated; if it's blocked internally, use a proprietary flushing compound.

T2/2 You may be able to repair the hose temporarily, as in T1/8, but it'll almost certainly mean a new one as soon as possible.

T2/3 Drive slower and don't labour the engine.

T4/1 You'll need a little extra pedal effort for braking but that's all. It may be possible to temporarily repair the vacuum hose as in T1/8.

T6/1 Remove the lamp lenses (see *In an Emergency*) and check for signs of rust. Where there's rust, scrape it off and apply a little petroleum jelly. Ensure that the screws securing the lamp body to the car are making good contact.

Car Jargon Explained

We hope there isn't much in this Handbook that you can't understand. However, most of us – particularly if we're trying to learn more about an unfamiliar subject – will sooner or later come across the odd word or phrase that needs explaining. This alphabetical list should help you understand the language spoken by your garage man, 'expert' neighbour, or that inevitable chap in the local...

A

Accelerator pump: A device attached to many *carburettors* which adds a spurt of extra fuel to the carburettor mixture when the accelerator pedal is suddenly pressed down.

Additives: Compounds which are added to petrol and lubricating oil to improve their quality and performance.

Advance and retard: A system for altering the ignition timing – the time in the firing cycle at which the ignition spark occurs. The spark timing is normally a few degrees of *crankshaft* revolution before the *piston* reaches the top of its stroke, and is expressed as so many degrees before top-dead-centre (BTDC). It's altered by devices in the *distributor* which detect changes in engine speed and load. Broadly speaking, as the engine speeds up the ignition is advanced (greater angle BTDC) but if there is a heavy engine load the ignition is retarded (smaller angle BTDC).

AF: An abbreviation of 'across flats', the way in which many nuts, bolt heads and spanners are now identified. It's preceded by an Imperial or metric unit of measurement – e.g.$\frac{1}{2}$ in AF or 11mm AF.

Air cooling: Alternative method of engine cooling in which no water is used. An engine-driven fan forces air at high velocity over the engine surfaces, which are enclosed by cowling. Normally an *oil cooler* is incorporated in the air flow to assist the rate of heat loss.

Alternator: A device for converting rotating mechanical energy into electrical energy. In modern cars, it has superseded the *dynamo* for charging the battery because of its much greater efficiency.

Ammeter: A device for measuring the current supplied to the battery from the *dynamo* or *alternator,* or drawn from the battery by the car lights, wipers, radio etc.

Antifreeze: A chemical compound mixed with the cooling system water to lower the temperature at which the coolant freezes.

Anti-roll bar A spring-steel bar mounted transversely across a car which counteracts the natural tendency for the car to lean over when cornering.

Aquaplaning: A phrase used to describe the action of a tyre skating across water.

Automatic transmission: A type of *gearbox* which selects the correct gear ratio automatically according to the engine speed and load.

B

Balljoint: A ball-and-socket type joint, used in steering and *suspension* systems, which permits relative movement in more than one plane.

Battery condition indicator: A voltmeter connected via the ignition switch to the car battery. Unlike an *ammeter* (which it's tending to supersede), it will warn you of impending battery failure.

Bearing: Metal or other hard wearing surface against which another part moves or rotates, and which is designed (and usually lubricated) to withstand the resulting friction.

Bendix drive: A device on many types of starter motor which allows the motor to be coupled to the *flywheel* for engine starting, then disengages when the engine commences to run.

BHP: See *Horsepower*

Big end: The end of a *connecting rod* which is attached to the *crankshaft*. It incorporates a *bearing* and transmits the linear movement of the con-rod to the motion of the crankshaft.

Bleed nipple (or valve): A hollow screw with a tapered seat which allows air or fluid to be bled out of a system when it is loosened.

Brake caliper: That part of a *disc brake* system which houses the *brake pads* and the *hydraulic* operating *pistons.*

Brake fade: A temporary loss of braking efficiency due to overheating of the brake friction material.

Brake pad: That part of a *disc brake* system which comprises the friction material and a metal backing plate.

Brake shoe: That part of a *drum brake* system which comprises the friction material and a curved metal former.

Breather: A device which allows fresh air into a system or allows contaminated air out.

Bucket tappet: A cup (or bucket) shaped piece of metal used in some engines to transmit the rotary *camshaft* movement to an up-and-down movement for *valve* operation.

Bump stop: A hard rubber device used in many *suspension* systems to prevent the moving parts from lifting the bodyframe during violent suspension movements.

C

Camber angle: The angle at which the front wheels are set from the vertical, when viewed from the front of the car. Positive camber is the amount in degrees by which the wheels are tilted outwards at the top.

Cam follower: A cylindrical piece of metal used to transmit the rotary *camshaft* movement to an up-and-down movement for *valve* operation.

Camshaft: A rotating shaft with lobes or cams used to operate the engine *valves.*

Carbon fibre leads: Black, string-like cores in the centre of some spark plug *HT* leads, which don't need separate radio and *TV* suppressors.

Carburettor: A device which is used to mix air and fuel in the correct proportions for all conditions of engine running. There are two main types: those with a number of fixed *jets,* and those with a single jet with a moving needle in it. In the former type, the different jets come into operation at different conditions of throttle opening, engine speed and engine load; in the latter type, the *needle jet* is controlled by a moving *piston,* the position of which depends on the amount of suction in the engine inlet *manifold.*

Castor angle: The angle between the front wheel pivot points and a vertical line when viewed from the side of the car. Positive castor is when the axis is inclined rearwards.

Centrifugal advance: System of ignition *advance and retard* incorporated in many *distributors* in which weights rotating on a shaft alter the ignition timing according to engine speed.

Choke: This has two common meanings. It is used to describe the device which shuts off some of the air in a *carburettor* during cold starting, and may be either manually or automatically operated. It's also used as a general term to describe the carburettor throttle bore.

Clutch: A friction device which allows two rotating devices to be coupled together smoothly, without the need for either rotating part to stop.

Coil spring: A spiral of spring steel used in many *suspension* systems.

Combustion chamber: Shaped area in the *cylinder head* into which the fuel/air mixture is compressed by the *piston* and in which combustion of the mixture is effected by the *spark plug.*

Compression ratio (CR): A term used to describe the amount by which the fuel/air mixture is compressed, and expressed as a number. For example, an 8.5 : 1 compression ratio means that the volume of fuel/air when the *piston* is at the bottom of its stroke is 8.5 times that when the piston is at the top of its stroke.

Compression tester: A special type of pressure gauge screwed into the *spark plug* hole which shows the *cylinder* compression when the engine is turning but not firing.

Condenser (capacitor): A device in the *distributor* which stores electrical energy and prevents excessive sparking at the *contact breaker* points.

Connecting rod: (con-rod): Rod in the engine connecting the *piston* to the *crankshaft.*

Constant velocity (CV) joint: A joint used in *drive-shafts,* where the speed of the input shaft is exactly the same as the speed of the output shaft at any angle of rotation. This does not occur in ordinary *universal joints.*

Contact breaker: The device in the *distributor* which comprises the electrical points (or contacts) and a cam which opens and closes them to operate the *HT* electrical circuit which provides the spark at the *spark plug.*

Crossflow cylinder head: A *cylinder head* in which the inlet and exhaust *manifolds* are on opposite sides.

Crossply tyre: A tyre whose construction is such that the weave of the fabric material layers is running diagonally in alternately opposite directions to a line around the circumference.

Cubic capacity: The total volume within the *cylinders*

103

which is swept by the *pistons*.

Cylinder head: That part of the engine which contains the *valves* and associated operating gear.

D

Damper: See *shock absorber*.

Dashpot: An oil-filled *cylinder* and *piston* used as a damping device in SU and Zenith/Stromberg CD type *carburettors*.

Dead axle (beam axle): The simplest form of axle, comprising a horizontal member attached to the chassis-frame by springs. This is used for the rear axle on some front-wheel-drive cars.

Decarbonizing ('decoking'): Removal of all carbon deposits from the *combustion chambers* of an engine.

De Dion axle: A rear axle comprising a cranked tube attached to the wheel hubs, with a separately mounted *differential* gear and *driveshafts*. *Suspension* is normally though *coil springs* between the wheel hubs and chassis frame.

Diaphragm: A stationary flexible membrane used in items such as fuel pumps. The diaphragm spring used in *clutches* is somewhat similar but is made from spring steel.

Diesel engine: An engine which relies upon the heat generated when compressing air to ignite the fuel, and which therefore doesn't need a *spark plug*. Diesel engines have much higher *compression ratios* than petrol engines, normally in the region of 20:1.

Differential: A system of gears (generally known as a crownwheel and pinion) which allows the *torque* from the *propeller shaft* to be applied to the driving wheels. The torque is divided proportionately between the driving wheels to permit one wheel to turn faster than the other if required, for example during cornering.

DIN: This stands for Deutsche Industrie Norm (roughly equivalent to the British Standards Institution) and lays down international standards for measuring output, performance, etc., of motor vehicles.

Disc brake: A braking system where a rotating disc is clamped between hydraulically operated friction pads.

Distributor: A collective term used to describe the *contact breaker, advance and retard* mechanisms, and associated parts of the *ignition system*.

Doughnut: A term used to describe the flexible rubber coupling used in some *driveshafts*.

Driveshaft: Name usually applied to the shaft (normally incorporating *universal* or *constant velocity joints*) which transmits the drive from a *transaxle* to one wheel; more commonly found in front-wheel-drive cars.

Drive train: A collective term used to describe the gearbox, propeller shaft, final drive and half-shafts of a front engine/rear wheel drive car.

Drum brake: A brake with friction linings on 'shoes' running inside a cylindrical drum attached to the wheel.

Dual circuit brakes: A *hydraulic* braking system comprising two separate fluid circuits so that if one circuit becomes inoperative, braking power is still available from the other circuit at a reduced efficiency.

Dwell angle: The number of degrees of *distributor* cam rotation during which the *contact breaker* points are closed during the ignition cycle of one *cylinder*. The angle is altered by adjusting the points gap, and is a more accurate way of setting-up the *ignition system*.

Dynamo: A device for converting rotating mechanical energy into electrical energy. This is a heavier, less efficient form of *generator* than the *alternator* and has largely been superseded by it during recent years.

• E

Earth strap: A flexible electrical connection between the battery and vehicle earth, or the engine/*gearbox* and chassis frame, to provide the return current-flow path in the electrical system.

Electrode: An electrical terminal or terminals, across which a spark occurs e.g., in a *spark plug* or *distributor* cap.

Electrolyte: A current-conducting solution of water and sulphuric acid, which is the liquid inside the car battery.

Electronic ignition: An *ignition system* incorporating electronic components which can produce a much greater spark voltage than in conventional systems.

Emission control: The prevention or reduction of the emission into the atmosphere of noxious fumes and gases from the engine and fuel tank of a motor vehicle. Required to varying degrees by the laws of different countries, it is effected by design and by special devices.

Epicyclic gears (planetary gears): A gear system used in many *automatic transmissions* where there is a centre 'sun' wheel around which smaller 'planet' gears inside a 'planet carrier' rotate.

Exhaust gas analyser: An instrument used for the measurement of pollutants (mainly carbon monoxide) in an exhaust system.

Expansion tank: A container used in many modern cooling systems to collect the overflow from the car's *radiator* as the coolant heats up and expands.

104

F

Filter: A device for extracting foreign particles from air or oil.

Final drive: A collective term (often expressed as a gearing ratio) for the crownwheel and pinion (see *Differential*).

Flat engine: Form of engine design in which the *cylinders* are positioned horizontally, usually with an equal number each side of a central *crankshaft*.

Float chamber: That part of a *carburettor* which contains a float and *needle valve* for controlling the fuel level.

Flywheel: A heavy rotating disc attached to the *crankshaft* used to smooth out the pulsating output from the *cylinders*.

Four stroke (cycle): A common term used to describe the four operating strokes of a *piston* in a conventional car engine. These are: (1) Induction - drawing in the fuel/air mixture as the piston goes down; (2) Compression of the fuel/air mixture as the piston rises; (3) Power stroke where the piston is forced down after the fuel/air mixture has been ignited by the *spark plug* and (4) Exhaust stroke where the piston rises and pushes the burnt gases out of the *cylinder*. During these operations, the inlet and exhaust *valves* are opened and closed at the correct moment to allow the fuel/air mixture in, the exhaust gases out, or to provide a gas-tight compression chamber.

Fuel injection: A method of injecting fuel into an engine. Used in *Diesel* engines, and also on some petrol engines as a replacement for the *carburettor*.

G

Gasket: Compressible material used between two metal surfaces to make a leakproof joint.

Gearbox: A group of gears and shafts installed in a metal housing. Physically, this is positioned between the *clutch* and the *differential,* and is used to multiply the engine *torque*.

Generator: See *alternator* and *dynamo*.

H

Half-shaft: A rotating shaft, two of which are used to transmit the drive from the *differential* to the wheels.

Hardy-Spicer joint (Hooke's or Cardan joint): See *Universal joint*.

Helical gears: Gears in which the teeth are cut at a slant across the circumference to give smoother meshing and quieter running.

Horsepower: A measurement of the rate of doing work. Where brake horsepower *(BHP)* is referred to, it's the amount of work required to stop a moving body.

HT: Abbreviation of high tension (meaning high voltage). Used in connection with the ignition system.

Hydraulic: A term used to describe the operation of a system by means of fluid pressure.

I

Ignition system: The electrical system which provides the spark to ignite the air/fuel mixture in the engine. Normally it comprises the battery, ignition coil, *distributor, (contact breaker and condenser),* ignition switch, *spark plugs* and wiring.

Ignition timing: See *Advance and retard*.

Inertia reel: Automatic type of safety belt which permits the wearer to move freely in normal use but which locks to give restraint on sensing either sudden deceleration of the car or sudden movement of the wearer.

In-line engine: Engine in which the *cylinders* are positioned in one row as distinct from being e.g. a *flat* or *vee* formation.

J

Jet: A calibrated nozzle or orifice in a *carburettor* through which fuel is drawn for mixing with air.

Jump leads: Heavy electric cables fitted with clips to enable a vehicle's battery to be connected to an external one for emergency starting.

K

Kerb weight: The weight of a car, unladen but ready to be driven, i.e. with enough fuel, oil etc. to travel an arbitrary distance.

Kickdown: A device used on *automatic transmissions* which allows a lower gear to be selected by flooring the accelerator.

Kingpin: A device which allows the front wheels of a car to swivel.

L

Laminated windscreen: A windscreen which has a thin plastic layer sandwiched between two layers of toughened glass. Its advantage is that it doesn't shatter or craze over when hit.

Leading shoe: Brake shoe of which the leading end (the one moved by the operating *cylinder)* is reached first by a given point on the drum during normal forward rotation. A simple single-cylinder *drum brake* will have one leading and one trailing (the opposite) shoe.

Leaf spring: A spring commonly used on cars with a *live axle,* comprising several long steel plates clamped together.

Little end: The smaller end of the *connecting rod* which is attached to the *piston.*

Live axle: An axle through which power is transmitted to the rear wheels.

Loom: A complete vehicle wiring system, or section thereof (e.g. front loom) comprising all the necessary cables of predetermined colours and lengths to wire up the various circuits.

LT: Abbreviation of low tension (meaning low voltage). Used in connection with *ignition systems.*

M

MacPherson strut: An independent front *suspension* system where the swivelling, springing and shock absorbing action of the wheel is dealt with by a single assembly.

Manifold: The device used for ducting the air/fuel mixture to the engine (inlet manifold), or the exhaust gases from the engine (exhaust manifold).

Master cylinder: A cylinder containing a *piston* and hydraulic fluid, directly coupled to a foot pedal (e.g. brake or clutch *master cylinder).* It's used for transmitting pressure to the brake or *clutch* operating mechanism.

Metallic paint: Paint finish incorporating minute particles of metal to give added lustre to the colour.

Multigrade: Lubricating oil whose *viscosity* covers that of several *monograde* oils, making it suitable for use over a wider range of operating conditions.

N

Needle bearing: Type of *bearing* in which needle or cone-shaped rollers are employed around the inner circumference, often used to reduce the space needed for the bearing.

Needle valve: A component of the *carburettor* which restricts the flow of fuel or fuel/air mixture according to its position relative to an orifice or *jet.*

Negative earth: Electrical system (now almost universally adopted) in which the negative terminal of the car battery is connected to the vehicle body, the polarity of all other electrical equipment being determined by this.

O

Octane rating: A scale rating introduced by the British Standards Institution for grading petrol.

OHC (overhead cam): Describes an engine in which the *camshaft* is situated above the *cylinder head,* and operates the *valve* gear directly without the need for *pushrods.*

OHV (overhead valve): Describes an engine which has its *valves* in the *cylinder head* (as in *OHC)* but suggests that the valve gear is operated via *pushrods* from a *camshaft* situated lower in the engine. Practically all modern car engines are OHV but are not necessarily OHC.

Oil cooler: Small *radiator* fitted in the lubricating oil circuit and sited in a cooling airflow to dissipate heat from the oil. Used mainly in higher-performance engines.

Overdrive: A device coupled to a car *gearbox* which raises the output gear ratio above the normal 1 : 1 of top gear. Also used to describe a top gear ratio of greater than 1 : 1 found in some cars.

Oversteer: A tendency for a car to turn more tightly into a corner than intended.

P

PCV (Positive crankcase ventilation): A system which allows fumes and vapours which build up in the crankcase to be drawn into the engine for burning.

Pinion: A gear with a small number of teeth which meshes with one having a larger number of teeth.

Pinking: A metallic noise from the engine often caused by the *ignition timing* being too far advanced. The noise is the result of pressure waves which cause the cylinder walls to vibrate, when the ignited fuel/air is compressed.

Piston: Cylindrical component which slides in a closely-fitting metal tube or *cylinder* and transmits pressure. The pistons in an engine, for example, compress the fuel/air mixture, transmit the combustion power to the *crankshaft,* and exhaust the burnt gases.

Piston ring: Hardened metal ring which is a spring fit in a groove running round the *piston* to ensure a close fit to the *cylinder* wall.

Positive earth: The opposite of *negative earth.*

Propeller shaft: The shaft which transmits the drive from the *gearbox* to the rear axle in front engine/rear drive.

Pushrod: A rod which is moved up and down by the rotary motion of the *camshaft* and operates the rocker arm in an OHV engine.

Q

Quarter light: A triangular window often mounted in the front door of a car.

Quartz-halogen bulb: A bulb with a quartz envelope (instead of glass) and a tungsten filament, and filled with one of the halogen group of gases (often iodine).

R

Rack and pinion: Simplest form of steering mechanism which uses a *pinion* gear to move a toothed rack.

Radial ply tyre: A type in which the tread plies are arranged laterally, at right angles to the circumferential plane.

Radiator: Cooling device, situated in an air flow and comprising a system of fine tubes and fins for rapid heat dissipation, through which engine coolant is passed.

Radius arms (rods): Locating arms sometimes used with a *live axle* to positively locate it in the fore-and-aft direction.

Recirculating ball steering: A derivation of *worm and nut* steering, where the steering shaft motion is transmitted to the steering linkage by balls running in the groove of a worm gear.

Rev-counter: See *tachometer.*

Rocker arm: A lever which rocks on a central pivot, one end is moved up and down by the *camshaft* action and the other end operates the inlet or exhaust *valve.*

Rotor arm: A rotating arm in the *distributor* which distributes the HT spark voltage to the correct *spark plug.*

Running on: A tendency for an engine to keep on running after the ignition has been switched off; it's often caused by a badly maintained engine, or use of an unsuitable grade of fuel.

S

SAE: Society of Automotive Engineers (of America). The SAE classification of oils is well known but, as with *DIN* standards, SAE covers a wide range of measuring output, performance, etc, of motor vehicles.

Safety rim: A special wheel rim shape which prevents a deflated tyre from rolling off the wheel.

Sealed beam: A sealed headlamp unit where the filament is an integral part and cannot be renewed separately. Although much more expensive than separate bulbs, the illumination does not deteriorate due to contamination.

Semi-elliptic spring: A *leaf spring* used for many car rear *suspension* systems.

Semi-trailing arm: A common form of independent rear *suspension* which allows the wheel carrier to be pivoted.

Servo: A device for multiplying the normal effort applied to a control. With a brake servo, this uses the suction created in the engine inlet *manifold* to act on a *diaphragm/pushrod* for additional braking effort; it's attached to the brake *hydraulic master cylinder.*

Shock absorber: A device for damping out the up-and-down movement of a car when the *suspension* hits a bump in the road.

Sonic-idle carburettor: A *carburettor* where the air used for the fuel/air mixture at idle speeds is mixed in a special by-pass tube which increases the pressure drop. The velocity of the mixture increases to above the speed of sound and at the same time it becomes very turbulent which improves the fuel/air atomization.

Spark plug: A device with a ceramic insulator and two electrodes on a common metal body which screws part-way into the engine *combustion chamber.* When the HT voltage is applied to the plug terminal, a spark jumps the air-gap at the electrodes.

Squab: Another name for a seat cushion.

Steel-braced tyre: Tyre in which an extra ply containing steel cords is incorporated to give added strength.

Steering arm (knuckle): Short arm on the rear face of the front *stub axle* to which the steering linkage connects.

Steering rack: See *Rack and pinion.*

Stroboscopic light: A light powered from the engine *ignition system* which is used for checking the ignition timing when the engine is running (i.e. dynamically).

Stroke: The total travel of the *piston* in the bore.

Stub axle: A short axle which carries the wheel only.

Sub-frame: A small frame or chassis which carries the *suspension,* and which in turn is connected to the car body.

107

Sump: The main oil container at the lowest part of an engine.

Suppressor: A device which is used to suppress or damp-out electrical interference caused by the *ignition system* or *generator,* wiper motor etc.

Suspension: A general term used to describe the links, springs and *dampers* with which the car body is suspended on the wheels.

Swing axle: A *suspension* arm which is pivoted near the centre-line of the car, and which gives the wheel a vertical swinging action about that pivot point.

Synchromesh: A device in a *gearbox* which synchronizes the speed of one gear shaft with another to produce smooth, noiseless engagement of the relative gears.

T

Tachometer: Also known as a rev counter, this indicates the engine speed in revolutions per minute (rpm).

Tappet: A term nowadays widely misused to refer to the adjustable part of the valvegear of an engine. True tappets are found only in the valvegear of older engines.

Thermostat: A device which is sensitive to changes in engine temperature, and opens up an additional path for coolant to flow when the engine has warmed up.

Tie-rod (track rod): A general term for a rod which provides location for a component, or between two components (as with steering linkage).

Timing chain: Metal flexible-link chain engaging on sprocket wheels and driving the *camshaft* from the *crankshaft* in an *OHV* engine.

Timing marks: Marks normally found on the *crankshaft* pulley or *flywheel* and used for setting the ignition firing point with respect to a particular *piston.*

Toe-in/toe-out: The amount by which the front wheels point inwards or outwards, expressed either as an angle or linear measurement.

Top dead centre (tdc): The point at which a piston is at the top of its stroke.

Torque: The turning effort generated by any rotating part.

Torque converter: A coupling where the driving *torque* is transmitted through oil. At low speeds there is very little transference of torque from the input to the output; as the input shaft speed increases, the direction of fluid flow within a system of vanes alters and torque from the input impeller is transferred to the output turbine. The higher the input speed, the closer the output speed approaches it, until they are virtually the same.

Torsion bar: A spring-steel bar which turns about its own axis, and is used in some independent front *suspension* systems.

Toughened windscreen: A windscreen which will shatter in a particular way to produce blunt-edged fragments or will craze over but remain intact. A zone-toughened windscreen has a zone in front of the driver which crazes into larger parts to reduce the loss of visibility which occurs with toughened windscreens, but is otherwise similar.

Track rod: A rod which connects the steering arms to the steering gear and/or steering idler gear.

Trailing arm: A form of independent *suspension* where the wheel is attached to a swinging arm, and is mounted to the rear of the arm pivot.

Transaxle: A form of combined *gearbox* and axle from which two shafts transmit the drive to the wheels.

Transmission: A general term for a *gearbox,* but very often used as an alternative for a *transaxle.*

Two-stroke (cycle): A common term used to describe the operation of an engine where each downward piston stroke is a power stroke. The fuel/air mixture is ported into the crankcase where it's compressed by the descending *piston* and 'pumped' through another port into the *combustion chamber.* As the piston rises, the mixture is compressed and ignited, which forces the piston down. The burnt gases flow from the exhaust port, but the piston is now compressing a further charge in the crankcase which repeats the cycle. The engine needs careful design to prevent the unburnt and burnt gases from mixing and, although not a feature of the simplest designs, in some versions a rotary or reed *valve* is incorporated to help achieve this.

U

Understeer: A tendency for a car to go straight on when turned into a corner.

Universal joint: A joint that can swivel in any direction whilst at the same time transmitting *torque.* It's commonly used in *propeller shafts* and *driveshafts,* but is not suitable for some applications because the input and output shaft speeds are not the same at all positions of angular rotation. The type in common use is known as a *Hardy-Spicer,* Hooke's or Cardan joint.

Unsprung weight: That part of a car which is not supported by the springs.

Upper cylinder lubricant (UCL): A type of light oil intended to be added to a car's fuel with the object of providing extra lubrication for the *cylinder* walls.

V

Vacuum advance: System of ignition *advance* and *retard* used in certain *distributors* where the vacuum in the engine intake *manifold* is transmitted to the distributor and acts on a *diaphragm* to alter the ignition timing according to throttle position.

Vacuum gauge; A device which indicates the amount of vacuum or suction in the inlet *manifold.*

Valve: A device which opens or closes to permit or stop gas flow into the engine.

Vee engine: Design in which the *cylinders* of an engine are set in two banks forming a V when viewed from one end. A V8, for example, consists of two such rows of four cylinders each.

Venturi: A streamlined restriction in the *carburettor* throttle bore which causes a low pressure to occur; this sucks fuel into the air stream to form a vapour suitable for combustion.

Viscosity: A term used to describe the resistance of a fluid to flow. When associated with lubricating oil it's given an *SAE* number, 10 being a very light oil and 140 being a very heavy oil.

Voltage regulator: A device which regulates the *generator* output to a predetermined level. For most alternator systems this is an integral part of the alternator itself, and therefore mainly applicable to *dynamo* systems. Regulators on later cars also have a device to regulate the charging current as well as the voltage.

W

Wankel engine: A rotary engine originally developed by Felix Wankel which has a triangular shaped rotor in an epitrochoidal housing (approximates in shape to a broad-waisted figure of eight). The engine has never proved popular in production cars in the UK.

Wheel balancing: Adding weights at the rim of a car wheel so that there are no out-of-balance forces.

Wishbone: An A-shaped *suspension* link, pivoted at the base of the A, and carrying a wheel at the apex. Normally mounted in an approximately horizontal plane.

Worm and nut steering: A steering system where the lower end of the steering column has a coarse screw thread on which a nut runs. The nut is attached to a spindle which carried the drop arm which, in turn, moves the steering linkage.

CONVERSION

Distance

Inches (in)	X 25.400	=	Millimetres (mm)
Feet (ft)	X 0.305	=	Metres (m)
Miles	X 1.609	=	Kilometres (km)
Millimetres (mm)	X 0.039	=	Inches (in)
Metres (m)	X 3.281	=	Feet (ft)
Kilometres (km)	X 0.621	=	Miles

Capacity

Inches, cubic (cu in/in^3)	X 16.387	=	Centimetres, cubic (cc/cm^3)
Fluid ounce, imperial (fl oz)	X 35.51	=	Centimetres, cubic (cc/cm^3)
Fluid ounce, US (fl oz)	X 29.57	=	Centimetres, cubic (cc/cm^3)
Pints, imperial (imp pt)	X 0.568	=	Litres (L)
Quarts, imperial (imp qt)	X 1.1365	=	Litres (L)
Quarts, imperial (imp qt)	X 1.201	=	Quart, US (US qt)
Quarts, US (US qt)	X 0.9463	=	Litres (L)
Quarts, US (US qt)	X 0.8326	=	Quarts, imperial (imp qt)
Gallons, imperial (imp gal)	X 4.546	=	Litres (L)
Gallons, imperial (imp gal)	X 1.201	=	Gallons, US (US gal)
Gallons, US (US gal)	X 3.7853	=	Litres (L)
Gallons, US (US gal)	X 0.8326	=	Gallons, imperial (imp gal)
Centimetres, cubic (cc/cm^3)	X 0.061	=	Inches, cubic (cu in/in^3)
Centimetres, cubic (cc/cm^3)	X 0.02816	=	Fluid ounces, imperial (fl oz)
Centimeters, cubic (cc/cm^3)	X 0.03381	=	Fluid ounces, US (fl oz)
Litres (L)	X 28.16	=	Fluid ounces, imperial (fl oz)
Litres (L)	X 33.81	=	Fluid ounces, US (fl oz)
Litres (L)	X 1.760	=	Pints, imperial (imp pt)
Litres (L)	X 0.8799	=	Quarts, imperial (imp qt)
Litres (L)	X 1.0567	=	Quarts, US (US qt)
Litres (L)	X 0.220	=	Gallons, imperial (imp gal)
Litres (L)	X 0.264	=	Gallons, US (US gal)

Area

Inches, square (in^2/sq in)	X 645.160	=	Millimetres, square (mm^2/sq mm)
Feet, square (ft^2/sq ft)	X 0.093	=	Metres, square (m^2/sq m)
Millimetres, square (mm^2/sq mm)	X 0.002	=	Inches, square (in^2/sq in)
Metres, square (m^2/sq m)	X 10.764	=	Feet square (ft^2/sq ft)

Weight

Ounces (oz)	X 28.350	=	Grammes (g)
Pounds (lbs)	X 0.454	=	Kilogrammes (kg)
Grammes (g)	X 0.035	=	Ounces (oz)
Kilogrammes (kg)	X 2.205	=	Pounds (lbs)
Kilogrammes (kg)	X 35.274	=	Ounces (oz)

FACTORS

Pressure

Pounds/sq in (psi/lb/sq in/ lb/in^2)	X 0.070	= Kilogrammes/sq cm (kg/sq cm)
Pounds/sq in (psi/lb/sq in/ lb/in^2)	X 0.068	= Atmospheres (atm)
Kilogrammes sq cm (kg/sq cm)	X 14.223	= Pounds/sq in (psi/lb/sq in/ lb/in^2)
Atmospheres (atm)	X 14.696	= Pounds/sq in (psi/lb/sq in/ lb/in^2)

Torque

Pound - inches (lbf in)	X 0.0115	= Kilogramme - metres (kgf m)
Pound - inches (lbf in)	X 0.0833	= Pound - feet (lbf ft)
Pound - feet (lbf ft)	X 12	= Pound - inches (lbf in)
Pound - feet (lbf ft)	X 0.138	= Kilogramme - metres (kgf m)
Pound - feet (lbf ft)	X 1.356	= Newton - metres (Nm)
Kilogramme - metres (kgf m)	X 86.796	= Pound - inches (lbf in)
Kilogramme - metres (kgf m)	X 7.233	= Pound - feet (lbf ft)
Newton - metres (Nm)	X. 0.738	= Pound - feet (lbf ft)
Newton - metres (Nm)	X 0.102	= Kilogramme - metres (kgf m)

Speed

Miles - hour (mph)	X 1.609	= Kilometres - hour (kph)
Feet - second	X 0.305	= Metres - second (m/s)
Kilometres - hour (kph)	X 0.621	= Miles - hour (mph)
Metres - second (m/s)	X 3.281	= Feet - second
Metres - second (m/s)	X 3.600	= Kilometres - hour (kph)

Consumption

Miles - gallon, imperial (mpg)	X 0.354	= Kilometres - litre (km/l)
Kilometres - litre (km/l)	X 2.825	= Miles - gallon, imperial (mpg)

Temperature

Centigrade (^{o}C) to Fahrenheit (^{o}F)

$$\frac{9}{5}\ ^oC + 32 = {}^oF$$

Fahrenheit (^{o}F) to Centigrade (^{o}C)

$$\frac{5}{9}\ (^oF - 32) = {}^oC$$

Index

Printed by
Haynes Publishing Group
Sparkford Yeovil Somerset
England